RODNEY STARK'S

Sociology

SECOND EDITION

STUDY GUIDE

Carol A. Mosher
Jefferson Community College

and

EXPERIMENTS IN SOCIOLOGY: FIVE COMPUTER SIMULATIONS

William Sims Bainbridge
Harvard University

Wadsworth Publishing Company
Belmont, California
A Division of Wadsworth, Inc.

to my parents: John and Rosalind Mosher

Printed in the United States of America

1 2 3 4 5 6 7 8 9 10—90 89 88 87

ISBN 0-534-06835-9

Contents

PREFACE
How to Use This Study Guide

This study guide is designed to aid your study of the second edition of Rodney Stark's <u>Sociology</u>. It is meant to complement the text, not substitute for it. The text is well written and contains a common thread that ties the chapters together; you will find it informative and lively reading. But even with a well-written text, students sometimes find it difficult to effectively focus their study and ferret out the most important information. This study guide will assist you in this process.

There is no foolproof way to study and no one way to use this study guide. This guide might be used in any (or all) of the following ways:

1. Before you read each chapter, the study guide can alert you to the key concepts, theories, and research studies discussed in the chapter. This preview will enable you to focus your attention effectively.

2. Throughout your reading and study, it can reinforce your knowledge of important topics.

3. After you complete each chapter, it can serve as a review and self-test to ensure that you understand the most important material.

4. Prior to an exam, it can serve as a review and refresher, alerting you to areas that may need further study.

You will want to develop a system that works best for you. Your professor or other students may be able to offer additional suggestions for effective use.

Format of the Study Guide

The text is divided into five parts, each containing between two and five chapters. (Individual professors may deviate from this format when designing courses.) Chapters in the study guide are grouped together to follow a format similar to that in the text but allow flexibility in the event of any deviation.

The study guide's twenty chapters directly correspond to the chapters in the text. Each chapter contains the following:

1. An overview that briefly highlights the main topics contained in the chapter.

2. A capsule summary that condenses the chapter into a few paragraphs. Key topics and concepts are underlined for easy reference.

3. A listing of key concepts. In addition, most chapters list key theories, research studies, and figures with specific page references for key concepts and research studies. These form the basis of sociology and sociological inquiry, and a thorough knowledge of them is essential for mastery of the material.

4. Completion, or fill-in-the-blank, questions that are drawn from all aspects of the chapter. The answers appear at the end of the chapter.

5. Multiple-choice questions that cover the entire chapter. Again, the answers are at the back of the chapter.

6. Essays that require a synthesis and application of the important material. Many of these use the key words described in the section on how to study. The first two essays in each chapter reflect the cognitive levels described in the introductory section on essay questions.

Following each group of chapters is a brief review of the chapters plus a suggestion for a special project designed to offer some creative ways of actually putting sociology to use with the information gained in that section. The directions for these projects are open-ended to allow flexibility and creativity and are meant as suggestions rather than specific assignments. You should consult your instructor for advice and direction before undertaking these projects. In addition, this study guide contains a short section on study techniques, describing some strategies for effective study and test taking. It is designed to be useful not only in your sociology course but in other college courses as well. Many of the completion and essay questions contained in this guide apply some of these techniques.

   Of course, study guides do have some limitations. No study guide can ever substitute for a thorough reading and comprehensive study of a text. That is not the purpose of a study guide, nor should it be. Many professors cover additional material in lectures, which obviously cannot be included in this guide; similarly, outside readings are often assigned, which must be studied separately. Occasionally, an individual professor may emphasize a specific area in the text in greater depth than it is treated here. This guide should be used as a resource and study aid, but it should not be relied on as the only tool for effective study. Nevertheless, this guide should assist you in your study and help you to appreciate the challenge and excitement of sociology.

Diskette to Accompany the Study Guide

Enclosed with the study guide is a diskette titled "Experiments in Sociology: Five Computer Simulations." The diskette, prepared by William Sims Bainbridge, Harvard University, can be used on an Apple+, IIc, IIe or IBM computer. The programs on the disk allow you to simulate real-life experiments in sociological research. Included are a study of juvenile delinquency, two studies of population growth, and two studies examining the spread of social movements through a community. All of the simulations are designed for introductory students but include options for more advanced students. You will be able to run the programs even if you have never used a microcomputer before. Complete directions for conducting the simulations make up the final chapter of this study guide. Your instructor may also ask you to turn in a report on some of your experiments.

Acknowledgments

I would like to thank Rodney Stark for asking me to write this study guide and Sheryl Fullerton, Liz Clayton, and Wadsworth Publishing Company for their assistance with this project. In addition I thank Jan Nichols for her editorial assistance and support.
    The section on using the SQ4R method was written by two specialists at Jefferson Community College. Nancy Hoover, coordinator of the Reading and Study Skills Center, provided me with a clear and straightforward explanation of the SQ4R method for studying textbooks. She willingly let me include it here. Sarah Dye, associate professor of English, provided me with extensive material on test-taking techniques. The section on effective test taking is drawn from her material. In addition Margo Elliott, assistant professor of psychology, wrote the section entitled "Essay Questions: Understanding Format" and helped write the essay questions. I am indebted to these colleagues for their information and assistance.

Carol Mosher

INTRODUCTION
Studying a Text: The SQ4R Method

Nancy Hoover
Coordinator of Reading, Study Skills Center
Jefferson Community College

Author's Note

Success in sociology or any other college course depends, in part, on your ability to study effectively. Good study techniques allow you to make the most of your study time and can ultimately lead to a better understanding of course material and better grades. Although no method of study works for all students in all courses, experts on study skills have devised several techniques that have proven successful. Of course, no study technique can compensate for failure to attend classes or failure to complete assigned work. These techniques can, however, allow you to retain more information and more effectively use your study time.

Many students, particularly freshmen, simply do not know how to study. They complain that they spend many hours studying, yet they perform poorly on exams and other assignments. I can appreciate their position since, as a freshman, I spent many hours trying to memorize whole passages from texts the night before an exam only to find that I had missed much of the important information and had forgotten most of what I had memorized. True, I had spent many hours studying, but they were, for the most part, wasted. I simply did not know how to study effectively. Once I learned basic study techniques, I actually spent fewer hours studying yet I learned more and received better grades.

This section offers some strategies for effective study by describing the SQ4R method for studying texts and providing suggestions for taking objective and essay tests. If you want to improve your study skills, investigate the resources available on your campus. Many colleges and universities have study skills centers and learning resources centers that are staffed by professionals trained in study skills; other campuses use specially trained counselors, tutors, or advisors to serve this function. Often professors or teaching assistants are more than willing to help. Most of these services are free of charge to students, but you must seek them out.

Carol Mosher

When an instructor gives that famous assignment, "Read Chapter Eight for next time," what does she mean? There are two jobs for the student implicit in that assignment. The first is to understand; the second is to remember. The instructor does not care how the information is received or stored, just as long as it is.

Among several steps to understanding and remembering, the first is to be able to organize ideas into main ideas and details and then to see the relationships between and among these ideas. For instance, if you drive into a gas station and ask the mechanic to tell you what is wrong with your car, you would be unhappy if he said, "I can name all the parts of the carburetor, something I learned in my auto mechanics class." And yet, this is the kind of learning many students do, mistaking it for the real thing. The problem with our mechanic is that he has concentrated on the details, thinking that they are as important as the main ideas; maybe he is unable to tell the difference between the two. This kind of learning is insufficient and does not reflect the way experts in the field think. If you are to pass tests prepared by your instructors, who are experts in their fields, you need to learn to think like them.

One excellent way to organize your textbook study is to use the SQ4R study technique, with its six steps of Survey, Question, Read, Recite, Rite, and Review.

Survey

The purpose of the survey step is to aid understanding and increase reading speed. Research shows that students who survey before they read material read it 24 percent faster than do those who do not survey. Why? Because if you know where you are going, you get there faster.

How do you survey? Read the title. Think about it for a few seconds. What do you know about it already? What do you think the chapter will include? Next, read the introduction, which provides an overview of the chapter. Read all the headings and subheadings. Look at pictures, charts, or graphs. Read the summary; see how it mirrors the introduction. Finally, read any questions, terms, or other important material at the end of the chapter. This entire process should take no more than three to five minutes. Now return to the beginning of the chapter and start the second step.

Question

The question step helps reveal the organization of the chapter and the relationship of details to main ideas, so that you will not end up like our auto mechanic, not seeing the forest for the trees. To do the question step, simply change headings into questions. For example, if the heading is "Racism," the obvious question is "What is racism?" Or if the subheading is "The Causes of Racism," the question would be "What are the causes of racism?" To begin relating ideas to each other, you can ask questions that relate subheadings to headings. If the heading is "Racism," and the subheading is "Forms of Discrimination," a good question would be "How does discrimination lead to racism?" or "Is discrimination a necessary part of racism?" Don't these sound like good test

questions? You can discover questions in headings, from study
guides, from class discussion, and throughout the text.

Read

Next, read to answer your questions. This reading is much
different from simply starting at the beginning of every chapter
and reading every word, hoping that important ideas somehow will
pop into your brain. As you look at your textbook, it is easy to
answer the question, "What are the causes of racism?" The answers
may be numbered, appear in boldface type, or be the first sentence
in each paragraph. A glance through your text will reveal how
easy it is to understand the structure of a textbook. Nearly all
textbooks are put together in a similar way, so once you
understand this method, you can apply it to every text.

Recite

Once you have located the answer in the text, your next job is to
put that information in short-term memory so that you will be able
to retrieve it later. The recite step will accomplish that for
you. How do you recite? Look at the question you have written,
look away, and answer the question <u>out</u> <u>loud</u> and <u>in</u> <u>your</u> <u>own</u> <u>words</u>.
Answering the question out loud helps you to remember the answer;
answering in your own words ensures that you understand the
answer.
      If you are unable to answer the question or you do not
understand it, mark it in your SQ4R notes so that you can listen
especially for that point when it is discussed in class. You
should do SQ4R with your chapter before you go to the class
discussion on it. If you have not prepared for the class, you
will be lost, trying to cope with new ideas, new vocabulary, and
disorganization all at once.
      When you have answered your question, simply move on to the
next heading or subheading, make up a question, and answer it out
loud and in your own words. Continue this process to the end of
the chapter.

Rite

Rite, a phonetic rendering of "write," means you should learn to
use cue notes. A cue is a word or phrase that helps you to recall
longer phrases. For example, "soc." might represent
"socialization" or some similar term that is too long to write out
every time it is used. "Soc?" might represent "What is the
definition of socialization?"
      As you form the questions and find the answers, write them
down in cue form. In this way, you can have all the questions and
answers from your chapter in a brief format.

The review step, the final task, is to ensure that what you have understood will be retrievable from your memory one, two, or several weeks after you study it. There are two important times to review. The first is before you finish a study session. Review what you have covered in that session by repeating the recite step. Ask yourself the question, look away, and answer it. If you cannot answer the question, look back at the answer, then ask yourself the question again. Repeat this process until you can answer the question.

The second review should take place once a week until you are tested on the material; again, use the recite process. This review should take no more than five to ten minutes.

SQ4R was formulated in the early 1940s. No one has discovered a better method for understanding and remembering textbook material. Research has demonstrated that use of SQ4R will ensure an average of 80 percent retention of textbook material. Many of you will do much better than that. Try it. The proof is in the performance.

Effective Test Taking

Most professors rely on periodic exams to assess students' knowledge of course material and determine final grades. Faithful study throughout the course is a necessary prerequisite for taking exams. Nevertheless, even the most well-prepared students often approach exams with some degree of anxiety and apprehension. Knowledge (and practice) of effective test-taking techniques can reduce some of this anxiety and increase the probability of receiving a high grade.

Exam questions typically fall into one of two categories: objective or subjective (essay) questions. Objective tests require short, specific answers. In contrast, subjective tests tend to require broader, in-depth answers. Objective questions typically do not rely on your instructor's personal judgment to determine whether or not they are correct. Subjective questions, however, are often graded on both form and content and depend, in part, on personal judgment to determine their quality. The answer to a subjective question may be technically correct yet not receive full credit if it does not provide enough information or is organized and written poorly.

Regardless of the type of test, certain strategies for preparing for and taking exams have proven effective. Although no technique can ensure success, research has shown that when the following practices are consistently followed they can be of great benefit to students.

Basic Strategies

Before the Exam: Preparation, of course, begins with basic study. If you have kept up with reading, class notes, and other assignments, preparation should be a matter of review rather than learning new material. These strategies are effective as the test draws near.

1. Take full advantage of any review time available from the instructor. Clear up any questions you may have about content and find out the exact structure of the test.

2. Review your SQ4R notes. Be alert to any problem areas.

3. Make up practice questions and answer them.

4. Use a "buddy" system. Compare your notes and practice questions with someone else in the class. You may have missed something that he or she noticed.

5. Get a good night's sleep the night before the test.

6. Bring all necessary materials and an extra pen and pencil.

7. Arrive at the testing center a few minutes early to obtain your favorite seat and get organized.

   Once the Test Has Begun:

1. Read and follow all directions. Be alert to possible choices of which questions to answer, time limits, point values, and so on.

2. Quickly read through all the questions. Budget your time.

3. Answer the questions you are sure of first. Go back to the others.

   Upon Completion:

1. Go back and check your answers.

2. Be certain you have not inadvertently omitted any questions and that you have followed the directions.

3. Check your spelling and grammar.

Objective Tests

Objective tests typically require short, specific answers testing your ability to recognize and recall information. Types of objective questions include multiple choice, matching, completion (fill-in-the-blanks), identification, and true/false.

When you take objective tests, it is especially important to follow specific directions since these exams are often scored by a computer or other device that has been programmed to accept only specific types of answers in specific places. By failing to use a pencil or making your pencil marks too light, for example, you can lose points even though your answer may be correct.

It is equally important to pay specific attention to point values of questions and sections. Objective tests often consist of a large number of questions that are worth only a few points each. Spending too much time on a question worth only two or three points can seriously jeopardize completion of the rest of the exam. It is better, in the long run, to miss a few points than run out of time and be forced to omit an entire section worth far more.

There are techniques for taking the various types of objective tests, which you should be able to learn at your campus learning center or other resource. You will find the information you gain worthwhile.

Subjective, or essay, questions are typically more general than objective questions and rely on your ability not only to recall or recognize information but also to synthesize, organize, and explain the information in depth. Because essay questions do tend to be broad, students often assume such questions require less study. In reality, however, they typically require more study because a deeper understanding of the material is required to answer the question successfully.

Many general test-taking strategies apply to subjective tests and should be followed. Reading and following directions is critical because students are often given a choice of questions to answer. Essay questions often contain specific directives indicating what to do and how to organize an answer. The following list includes some common directives and their meanings:

Analyze: break into parts
Choose: select
Comment: similar to "discuss"
Compare: show similarities or similarities and differences
Contrast: show differences
Compare and contrast: show similarities and differences
Criticize: examine the pro and con positions and give your
         judgment
Define: give the meaning
Discuss: give as much information as you can
Evaluate: make a judgment and include the reasons that led to
        this judgment
Explain: give reasons
Illustrate: give examples
Interrelate: show relationships among
List: make the major points stand out clearly
Show: explain
State: give the information
Trace: show step-by-step development

You should also be alert to key words such as <u>after</u>, <u>before</u>, and <u>briefly</u> and phrases such as <u>two out of three</u>, which specify and limit. By alerting yourself to these directives and key words, you can better organize your essay and avoid wasting time by providing information that is not required. The essay items in this study guide use several of these directives and key words. Note them as you use this guide and take essay exams.

Outline your answer before actually writing the essay to be certain you have included all the major points in logical order. If you run out of time, some instructors will give partial credit for material in outline form. Unless you are told differently, essays should be in paragraph form with a thesis sentence and a conclusion. Remember, many instructors also grade on spelling and punctuation, as well as on organization, so be certain your essay is grammatically correct. Your answer will also be enhanced if you use the correct terminology of your discipline.

I hope that you will find these techniques and strategies helpful. Learning and using proper study techniques will benefit you throughout your academic and professional career.

Essay Questions: Understanding Format

Margo Elliott

Often students complain that even though they studied their material diligently, they still did not do well on their exams. This is particularly true in the case of essay questions. Students may feel that the instructor asked the "wrong" questions or stated them in a manner that was confusing or ambiguous.

More than likely this problem is due in part to the way students learn information and in part to how they understand information. Memorizing facts, theories, and data is insufficient in answering questions that require anything more than simple knowledge. For facts to be useful, you must be able to understand and apply those facts; this is what your instructors are testing. Psychologists have suggested that there are different levels of comprehension and that these levels can be represented by a categorization scheme or taxonomy. One such system is Bloom's stage theory of cognitive development.* Bloom suggests that there are six stages of understanding, each stage becoming successively more difficult and requiring a higher level of comprehension.

Stage one is the knowledge level. Knowledge questions require simple memorization and recall of various terms, theories, and research.

Stage two is the level of comprehension, and it involves the ability to understand nonliteral statements, such as examples, symbolism, and metaphors.

Stage three, the application level, requires applying concepts or scientific terminology.

The fourth stage is analysis and it uses the ability to recognize assumptions, to comprehend relationships, and to distinguish facts from hypotheses.

Stages five and six involve synthesis and evaluation, respectively. These levels generally require a greater knowledge base of the discipline than is typically required in an introductory course. These cognitive abilities would more likely be used in upper-level and graduate work and will therefore not be discussed here.

To further clarify these stages, let's use a simple fictitious example:

Animal specialists have developed two methods you can use to teach your dog not to bark at the letter carrier. The first method (A) involves verbal punishment and reprimand when your dog (Sadie) barks at the letter carrier. The second method (B) utilizes reward and verbal praise when Sadie does not bark at the letter carrier. After months of training, the specialists concluded that while both methods worked, method B was more effective than method A.

Assume that you have read a text that presented a detailed account of the preceding research. Here are sample questions your instructor might ask which reflect the various levels. Notice how

*Benjamin S. Bloom, <u>Cognitive Domain</u> (New York: McKay, 1969).

9

a greater degree of understanding is reflected in the increasing complexity of the questions.

Level I: Knowledge

1. What is the dog's name?

2. How many methods of training were discussed?

(Note that these questions are simple recall of concrete and specific information.)

Level II: Comprehension

1. Explain the two methods of training.

2. Give examples of appropriate reward and punishment for Sadie.

(Note the slightly higher level of skills involved in answering these questions. Be sure to understand that explain does not mean list.)

Level III: Application

1. Using either method A or B, devise a training program for a dog that barks at the letter carrier.

2. How might these methods be used for training Sadie to shake hands?

(Note that these questions require applying an understanding of concepts and facts.)

Level IV: Analysis

1. Explain why method B is a more successful training program than method A.

2. Can these methods be generalized to child-rearing techniques? Be specific.

(Note that this level requires individual thought.)

When preparing to study for exams, you will want to be alert to these various forms that content, or essay, questions can take. You might also ask your instructor if he or she would be willing to provide sample questions.

In the essay sections of each chapter you will find questions that reflect the various levels. You may wish to refer back to this section when preparing those questions.

CHAPTER 1
Groups and Relationships:
A Sociological Sampler

Overview

This chapter introduces the discipline of sociology: what it
studies and how it differs from other social sciences. It opens
with a discussion of the beginnings of sociology in the works of
moral statisticians such as Quételet and Morselli. Special
attention is paid to Durkheim's work in the area of suicide. It
then discusses the main focus of sociology--the group--and
distinguishes among types of groups. It introduces both micro
and macro sociology. (The trend from micro to macro will be a
major focus of this text.) It also discusses the scientific
nature of sociology and highlights some of the challenges,
drawbacks, and advantages of studying self-aware subjects. Chapter
1 offers some examples of research techniques such as unobtrusive
measures and validation research designed to minimize potential
problems. Stanley Milgram's "small world" research and MacKay's
study of parallel networks are highlighted as the "over-the-
shoulder" examples. (The "over-the-shoulder" items will be an
essential feature of other chapters.) The chapter concludes with
a brief discussion of the historical background of sociology and
a discussion of the compatibility of the doctrine of free will
and the social sciences.

Capsule Summary

Sociology began when <u>moral statisticians</u> such as Quételet and
<u>Morselli</u> began to study suicide rates in Europe. <u>Emile Durkheim</u>
further elaborated upon these data and argued that high suicide
rates reflect a <u>weakness in the web of relationships among
members of a society</u>. Gradually the study of moral statistics
began to uncover the <u>social causes of individual behavior</u> and
<u>sociology</u> was born.
    <u>Sociology</u> shares with the other <u>social sciences</u> an interest
in human behavior. It differs from the other social sciences in
its primary focus: <u>the patterns and processes of human social
relations</u>. The study of <u>group behavior</u> is thus of major concern
to sociologists. Indeed, sociology is often divided into <u>micro</u>
and <u>macro</u> sociology depending on the size of the group studied.
    Groups may be large or small, but they all share the common
characteristic of <u>social relations among members</u>. The smallest
possible group is the <u>dyad</u> or group of two. <u>Triads</u> (groups of
three) are of particular interest to sociologists because they
often demonstrate the rules of <u>transitivity</u> and <u>coalition
formation</u>. The patterns of social relations among members of a
group are termed <u>networks</u>. <u>Sociograms</u> are used to study the
structure of networks. Groups vary not only in size but also in
the degree of intimacy shared by members. Groups in which the

members share a good deal of intimacy are termed <u>primary groups</u>; those in which relationships are more impersonal are termed <u>secondary groups</u>.

Science is a method of discovery. Social scientists are in a unique position among scientists because their subjects are self-aware. <u>Unobtrusive measures</u> provide an interesting technique for studying self-aware subjects. <u>Validation research</u> is often employed to test the accuracy of data. Although bias does present a potential problem in sociological research, the nature of scientific inquiry minimizes this bias. Science often seeks to challenge previous assumptions and theories.

<u>Mass society theorists</u> were concerned that <u>modernization</u> had led to a breakdown in social relationships among urban dwellers. (The theme of modernization will be dealt with extensively in later chapters.) Milgram's "small world" research and MacKay's study of <u>parallel networks</u> challenged many of these assumptions.

The origins of the social sciences can be traced to philosophy, but it was not until recently that research was conducted in the social sciences. Economist <u>Adam Smith</u> (1776) may be considered the first real social scientist. <u>Auguste Comte</u> used the term <u>sociology</u> in the 1830s, and early European sociologists included <u>Spenser</u>, <u>Tonnies</u>, and <u>Durkheim</u>. <u>Albion Small</u> and <u>W.E.B. DuBois</u> were important in the development of sociology in <u>America</u>.

The doctrine of <u>free will</u> is compatible with the social sciences even though on the surface it may appear contradictory. All social science theories assume that humans possess the ability to reason and make choices. These choices are, however, predictable since people will choose what they find rewarding given their circumstances, information, and preferences.

Key Concepts

You should be able to explain the concepts in the following list. You should also be able to cite several examples of each concept. The page number after each concept indicates where the concept is introduced.

Moral statistics	5	Network	10
Sociology	7	Sociogram	10
Social science	7	Internal faction (clique)	10
Micro sociology	7	Primary group	12
Macro sociology	7	Secondary group	12
Group	8	Unobtrusive measure	15
Aggregate	8	Validation research	16
Dyad	8	Self-report studies	16
Triad	8	Chains of attachments	19
Transitivity rule	8	Parallel networks	21
Intransitive triad	10	Religious determinism	25
Coalition	10	(fatalism)	
Power	10	Free will	25

Key Research Studies

Be familiar with both the methodology and the results of the
research studies cited here.

> Durkheim: <u>Suicide</u> - study of suicide rates based on
> Morselli's data   6
> Bainbridge and Stark: use of unobtrusive measures in
> studying geographical patterns in
> metaphysical beliefs and practices
> 14
> Hirschi: delinquency study using validation research   17
> Milgram: "small world" research on networks   20
> J. Ross MacKay: parallel social networks in Canada   21

Key Figures

You should be able to associate each person with his contribution.

> Adolphe Quetelet: founder of moral statistics
> Henry Morselli: gathered statistics on suicide
> Emile Durkheim: wrote <u>Suicide</u> and argued that high suicide
> rates reflect a weakness in social
> relationships
> Charles H. Cooley: coined the term <u>primary group</u>
> Adam Smith: economist and first social scientist
> Auguste Comte: coined the term <u>sociology</u>
> Herbert Spenser: published <u>Principles of Sociology</u>
> Ferdinand Tonnies: published <u>Gemeinschaft und Gesellschaft</u>
> Albion Small: founded first sociology department in America
> at the University of Chicago
> W.E.B. DuBois: created a sociological laboratory and directed
> the Atlanta University Conferences

Key Theories

Be prepared to explain the assumptions of these theories and, when
applicable, to cite related research findings.

> Micro sociology
> Macro sociology
> Free will

Completion

Although each statement has only one blank, some may require two
or more words for completion.

1.   The founder of moral statistics was _____.

2.   Durkheim argued that _____ suicide rates reflect weaknesses in the web of relationships among members of society.

3.   The topic of sociology is _____.

4.   _____ sociologists tend to focus on large groups and whole societies.

5.   The smallest social group is a _____.

6.   "Any friend of yours is a friend of mine" demonstrates the rule of _____.

7.   The ability to get one's way over the opposition of others is termed _____.

8.   The patterns of relationships among members of a group are often called _____.

9.   _____ groups are characterized by great intimacy among members.

10. _____ measures obtain information without disturbing the objects of the research.

11. Comparison of results when different measures are used is one way to assess the _____ of sociological data.

12. Milgram and MacKay both studied the existence of _____.

13. MacKay discovered that language barriers within Canada are much _____ than are national boundaries.

14. The essence of the scientific method is _____.

15. The proper approach to research is to try to _____ those things that the researcher actually believes to be true.

16. Personal bias is possibly a more serious problem in _____ than for natural or physical sciences.

17. Scientific explanations must take the form of theories and these must be the object of testing by _____.

18. The term sociology was first suggested by _____.

19. _____ created a sociological laboratory and directed the Atlanta University Conferences.

20. The doctrine of _____ argues that humans possess the capacity for choosing among alternatives and, therefore, can be held responsible for the choices they make.

1. Nineteenth-century statistics comparing suicide rates from one nation to another showed that:
   a. the rates were extremely stable year to year
   b. the rates varied little from one nation to another
   c. during the nineteenth century the rates declined sharply
   d. all of the above
   e. none of the above

2. Emile Durkheim argued that:
   a. traditional rural societies were deficient in the kinds of warm interpersonal relationships typical of modern societies
   b. high suicide rates reflect a weakness in an individual's personality
   c. high suicide rates reflect weaknesses in the web of relationships among members of society
   d. a and c
   e. a and b

3. Sociologists differ from psychologists in that psychologists have typically studied:
   a. industrial societies
   b. illegal behavior
   c. preliterate societies
   d. political organization
   e. individual behavior

4. The primary subject of sociology is:
   a. the individual
   b. the group
   c. preliterate societies
   d. illegal behavior
   e. political organization

5. The main difference between micro sociology and macro sociology is:
   a. the size of the group studied
   b. the research method used
   c. the training of the researcher
   d. the degree of industrialization achieved by the group studied
   e. the presence of self-aware subjects in micro sociology

6. The social sciences include:
   a. anthropology
   b. political science
   c. sociology
   d. a and c
   e. all of the above

7. Intransitive triads:
   a. are demonstrated by the statement "any friend of yours is a friend of mine"
   b. are unstable and usually break up
   c. may lead to coalition formation--two against one
   d. all of the above
   e. b and c

8. A triad is:
   a. a group of three
   b. the smallest sociological group
   c. always intransitive and unstable
   d. all of the above
   e. a and c

9. Primary group members:
   a. share a good deal of intimacy with each other
   b. gain much of their self-esteem from their groups
   c. often refer to themselves as "we"
   d. a and c
   e. all of the above

10. Which of the following would most likely not be considered a primary group?
    a. a political party
    b. a group of intimate friends
    c. a family
    d. b and c
    e. none of the above

11. When researchers test data against some independent standard of accuracy, they are:
    a. utilizing an unobtrusive measure
    b. conducting validation research
    c. using self-reports
    d. a and c
    e. none of the above

12. In his study of delinquency, Travis Hirschi:
    a. utilized self-reports
    b. conducted validation research
    c. used both interviews and questionnaires
    d. a and b
    e. all of the above

13. Milgram's "small world" research:
    a. lent considerable support to mass society theories
    b. found that most of the letters did not reach their designated receiver
    c. discovered that people throughout the country were united by "chains of attachment"
    d. discovered a very strong interest in astrology in the Far West
    e. a and b

14. The researcher who arranged to have auto mechanics note the position of the radio dials in cars they serviced in order to ascertain what stations people listened to while driving used:
    a. an unobtrusive measure
    b. validation research
    c. self-reported behavior studies
    d. b and c
    e. all of the above

15. The term sociology was first suggested by:
    a. Adolphe Quetelet
    b. Auguste Comte
    c. Emile Durkheim
    d. Charles H. Cooley
    e. Albion Small

16. Which of the following early sociologists is not correctly paired with his contribution?
    a. Ferdinand Tonnies: published Gemeinschaft und Gesellschaft
    b. Emile Durkheim: suggested the term sociology
    c. Albion Small: founder of the first sociology department in North America
    d. a and b
    e. b and c

17. The author considers the field of sociology to be about _____ years old.
    a. 2,000
    b. 300
    c. 200
    d. 100
    e. 20

18. Reasons for the existence of parallel networks include:
    a. racism
    b. language
    c. distance
    d. a and b
    e. all of the above

19. Which of the following statements is/are true?
    a. The essence of the scientific method is systematic skepticism.
    b. The purpose of scientific research is to test what we believe about the world.
    c. Since bias is a problem in sociological research, sociologists must completely rid themselves of personal biases before beginning research.
    d. a and b
    e. all of the above

20. The doctrine of free will:
    a. is incompatible with the social sciences
    b. assumes that humans have the ability to reason and to make choices
    c. assumes that people will seek those things they find rewarding and will avoid those they find unrewarding
    d. b and c
    e. all of the above

Essay

In each chapter questions 1 and 2 are designed to reflect the cognitive levels described in the Introduction. In each case the general topic in question is divided into three smaller questions, each requiring a different level of understanding. Some questions tap the levels of knowledge, comprehension, and application while others tap comprehension, application, and analyses. The level is indicated in parentheses. You might wish to refer back to the Introduction for a more detailed explanation of the cognitive level in question. Admittedly, some of these essays are fairly long and difficult, but by using them for practice you should be able to test yourself on how well you have mastered the material in question.

1. A. Name some research techniques used to study self-aware subjects. (knowledge)
   B. Explain these research techniques. (comprehension)
   C. Design a simple study that uses one of the above techniques. (application)

2. A. Name some assumptions of mass society theorists. (knowledge)
   B. Explain Milgram's research. (comprehension)
   C. Show how Milgram's results did or did not support mass society theory. (analysis)

3. Trace the development of the social sciences from their origins in philosophy to the present.

4. Discuss the principles of transitivity and coalition formation. Explain how the study of networks is relevant to both micro and macro sociology.

5. Explain the following statement: "It is only because people's choices are predictable that it is possible to claim that they have free will."

Completion

1. Adolphe Quetelet
2. high
3. interpersonal relationships (or groups)
4. Macro
5. dyad
6. transitivity
7. power
8. social networks
9. Primary
10. Unobtrusive
11. validity
12. social networks
13. less powerful
14. systematic skepticism
15. disprove
16. social
17. systematic research
18. Auguste Comte
19. W.E.B. DuBois
20. free will

Multiple Choice

1.	a	11.	b
2.	c	12.	e
3.	e	13.	c
4.	b	14.	a
5.	a	15.	b
6.	e	16.	b
7.	e	17.	d
8.	a	18.	e
9.	e	19.	d
10.	a	20.	d

CHAPTER 2
Using Sociological Concepts:
A Comparative Study of Ethnic Mobility

Overview

This chapter opens with a discussion of the importance of concepts
in science. It then discusses two important concepts in
sociology: society and culture. Patterns of intergroup relations
are discussed, social stratification is introduced, and the
concepts of class, mobility, achieved status, and ascribed status
are explained. Chapter 2 introduces cultural components such as
norms, values, and roles. Zborowski and Herzog's study of Jewish
immigrants is highlighted as the "over-the-shoulder" example; the
works of Covello and Steinberg are also discussed. The chapter
closes with a look at the importance of reference groups.
     Note: Many concepts central to sociology are introduced in
this chapter. A thorough understanding of these concepts will
enhance your understanding of later chapters.

Capsule Summary

Concepts are used in science to classify sets of things that are
alike. They are abstractions that serve as building blocks of
science and allow for a common vocabulary.
     Society and culture are essential concepts in sociology. A
society is a group of people characterized by social
relationships, relative self-sufficiency and independence,
duration over time, a physical location, and a common culture.
Culture, on the other hand, is the pattern of living that people
have developed and handed down through generations. Norms,
values, and roles are important components of culture. Norms
refer to rules or guidelines for behavior while values serve as
standards for assessing the desirability or undesirability of
something; norms and values are often related. Roles refer to
collections of norms associated with particular positions in
society. Cultures differ not only in their actual norms, values,
and roles but also in the relative importance attached to them.
     Social stratification refers to the unequal distribution of
rewards among members of a society. Societies are "layered" and
these layers constitute classes: groups of people sharing a
similar position (or status) in a society. Movement within the
stratification system is termed mobility, and the direction it
takes may be upward or downward. Position (status) within the
stratification system may be based on either achievement or
ascription.
     Whenever members of one culture immigrate to another,
different patterns of intergroup relations may occur. If the
immigrant group gives up its old culture and totally adopts the
new, assimilation has occurred. If members of the new culture
resist full acceptance of the immigrant group, then prejudice and

discrimination against the immigrant group may result. In such cases, the immigrant group may become a subordinate group in the new culture. In other cases, accommodation may occur, which results in cultural pluralism. Often the immigrant group becomes a subculture within the new culture.

During the nineteenth and twentieth centuries many immigrant groups were the objects of prejudice and discrimination when they arrived in the United States and Canada. The experiences of both Jewish and Italian immigrants to the United States provide interesting examples of cultural differences. Zborowski and Herzog studied shtetl life in Europe to gain information on the cultural background of Jewish immigrants. They concluded that this background was a major factor in facilitating upward mobility after immigration. Steinberg further investigated this area and found that the occupational background of Jewish immigrants also facilitated upward mobility. In his study of Italian immigrants, Covello found that their cultural background initially served as a deterrent to upward mobility. Their reference group identification probably was also a factor because most Italian immigrants considered their reference group to be those who remained in Italy. Thus, the research studies indicate that differences in cultural background may partly explain the differing rates of initial upward mobility between Jewish and Italian immigrants. Recent data indicate that prejudice against Jews (anti-Semitism) and Italians in the United States and Canada seems to have diminished markedly as a result of assimilation (particularly intermarriage) and accommodation.

Key Concepts

You should be able to explain the concepts listed here, as well as be able to cite several examples of each concept.

Concept	30	Discrimination	36
Society	32	Value	36
Culture	33	Norm	36
Technology	34	Role	37
Stratification	35	Assimilation	37
Class	35	Accommodation	39
Status	35	Cultural pluralism	39
Upward mobility	35	Subculture	40
Downward mobility	35	Anti-Semitism	43
Achieved status	35	Ghetto	46
Ascribed status	36	Reference group	56
Prejudice	36		

Key Research Studies

You should be familiar with both the methodology and the results of the following research studies.

Glock and Stark, Stark and others: anti-Semitism in the
                                        United States   43
Zborowski and Herzog: cultural backgrounds of Jewish
                    immigrants   45
Covello: cultural background of Italian immigrants   48
Steinberg: cultural and occupational backgrounds of Jewish
                    immigrants   50

Completion

1. _____ are abstractions that are used to classify sets of things that are alike.

2. A(n) _____ is a group of people who are united by special relations and is relatively self-sufficient and independent.

3. _____ is the complex pattern of living that humans have developed and pass from generation to generation.

4. Everything that humans learn is _____.

5. _____ refers to the various materials and objects that people learn to use.

6. Stratification is the _____ distribution of rewards among members of a society.

7. When a lawyer's daughter becomes a factory worker, we can say she has experienced _____ mobility.

8. _____ statuses are derived from inheritance, whereas _____ statuses are derived from individual merit.

9. _____ refers to negative attitudes toward a group, while _____ refers to actions taken against a group.

10. Norms are _____ governing behavior.

11. The _____ of a culture identify its ideals.

12. A(n) _____ is a collection of norms associated with a particular position in a society.

13. The process of exchanging one culture for another is termed _____.

14. _____ occurs when accommodation results in the continued existence of several distinctive cultures within a society.

15. A distinctive set of beliefs, morals, customs, and the like developed or maintained by a group within a larger society is called a(n) _____.

16. Prejudice against Jews is termed _____.

17. Marrying someone of another ethnic background is called _____.

18. Zborowski and Herzog found that the cultural background of Jews stressed _____ as an important value.

19. Covello found that the cultural background of Italian immigrants did not serve to foster their achievement of _____.

20. Groups that individuals identify with and whose norms and values serve as their basis for self-judgment are termed _____.

_____

Multiple Choice

1. Which of the following statements is/are true?
   a. Concepts are names used to identify some set or class of things that are said to be alike.
   b. Scientific concepts are concrete; they identify things, not ideas.
   c. Concepts are the building blocks of any science.
   d. a and c
   e. all of the above

2. Characteristics of societies include:
   a. a definite physical location
   b. relative self-sufficiency and independence
   c. existence over time
   d. a and c
   e. all of the above

3. Culture is:
   a. everything that humans learn
   b. a group of people united by social relationships
   c. often synonymous with nation
   d. a and c
   e. all of the above

4. When a factory worker's child becomes a physician we say that he or she has experienced:
    a. upward mobility
    b. downward mobility
    c. circular mobility
    d. horizontal mobility
    e. none of the above

5. Ascribed statuses may be based on:
    a. family background
    b. individual merit
    c. genetic inheritance
    d. a and c
    e. all of the above

6. The caste system in India:
    a. is an extreme example of a stratification system based on achieved status
    b. is based on an individual's ability or merit
    c. is an extreme example of a stratification system based on ascribed status
    d. a and b
    e. all of the above

7. Rules governing behavior are termed _____.
    a. values
    b. beliefs
    c. norms
    d. roles
    e. none of the above

8. Which of the following statements is/are true?
    a. The values of a culture identify its ideals.
    b. Norms are quite general whereas values are specific.
    c. Values justify the norms.
    d. a and c
    e. all of the above

9. _____ refers to negative attitudes toward a group, while _____ refers to negative actions against a group.
    a. Prejudice, discrimination
    b. Discrimination, prejudice
    c. Prejudice, accommodation
    d. Subordination, discrimination
    e. Prejudice, assimilation

10. Which of the following statements is/are true?
    a. Social life is structured by roles.
    b. Cultures differ in their evaluation of various roles.
    c. Some roles are thought to be more demanding than others.
    d. b and c
    e. all of the above

11. The process of exchanging one culture for another
    a. assimilation
    b. accommodation
    c. cultural pluralism
    d. discrimination
    e. cultural exchange

12. The existence of different religions side by side in the United States today is an example of:
    a. cultural pluralism
    b. assimilation
    c. subordinate groups
    d. discrimination
    e. cultural lag

13. Historically in America the _____ have been the targets of prejudice and discrimination.
    a. Jews
    b. Irish
    c. Poles
    d. a and c
    e. all of the above

14. Anti-Semitism refers to prejudice against _____.
    a. Italians
    b. Blacks
    c. Jews
    d. Roman Catholics
    e. none of the above

15. According to Covello, immigrants from Southern Italy brought with them to America:
    a. a "cult of scholarship" and emphasis on learning
    b. the belief that school was harmful and a threat to family loyalty
    c. extensive training in the professional and middle-class occupations
    d. a and c
    e. none of the above

16. Steinberg found that many of the immigrant Jews:
    a. had been farmers and hence could only find employment in unskilled occupations
    b. were trained in skilled and professional occupations
    c. were single men who planned to return to their families in Europe
    d. a and c
    e. none of the above

co Jewish immigrants, Italian immigrants:

achieved upward mobility

y learned English and assimilated into American

ure

me with their families and planned to stay in America

of the above

e. f the above

18. Studies by Stark and others on anti-Semitism found that by the middle and late 1960s:
    a. prejudice against Jews was increasing
    b. prejudice against Jews had declined greatly
    c. prejudice against Italians had declined
    d. prejudice against Italians had increased
    e. none of the above

19. Which of the following statements is <u>not</u> true?
    a. A major aspect of assimilation is intermarriage.
    b. Despite substantial assimilation, large Jewish and Italian subcultures still exist in the United States and Canada.
    c. Jewish intermarriage rates in Canada and the United States are higher than those of Italians.
    d. A and b are not true.
    c. A and c are not true.

20. Reference groups:
    a. are groups that individuals identify with
    b. are the people whose approval counts most with us
    c. must be present to influence a person's behavior
    d. a and b
    e. all of the above

Essay

1. A. Describe the research findings of Zborowski and Herzog and of Steinberg. (knowledge)
   B. Do you feel the cultural backgrounds of other minorities have influenced their mobility? Give specific examples. (comprehension)
   C. Contrast the cultural backgrounds of Jewish and Italian immigrants and show how these backgrounds influenced their mobility. (analysis)

2. A. Briefly explain the terms <u>norm</u>, <u>value</u>, and <u>role</u>. (knowledge)
   B. Give two examples of the above terms. (comprehension)
   C. Interrelate these concepts using specific examples. (analysis)

3. Discuss some of the characteristics and uses of scientific concepts.

4. Distinguish between society and culture and discuss the characteristics of each.

5. Discuss some patterns of intergroup relations that might occur when immigrant groups arrive in a new culture. Give examples from American history.

Answers

Completion

1.	Concepts	11.	values
2.	society	12.	role
3.	Culture	13.	assimilation
4.	culture	14.	Cultural pluralism
5.	Technology	15.	subculture
6.	unequal	16.	anti-Semitism
7.	downward	17.	intermarriage
8.	Ascribed, achieved	18.	education
9.	Prejudice, discrimination	19.	upward mobility
10.	rules	20.	reference groups

Multiple Choice

1.	d	11.	a
2.	e	12.	a
3.	a	13.	e
4.	a	14.	c
5.	d	15.	b
6.	c	16.	b
7.	c	17.	e
8.	d	18.	b
9.	a	19.	d
10.	e	20.	d

CHAPTER 3
Micro Sociology:
Choice and Interaction

Overview

Chapter 3 opens with a discussion of scientific theories. It
then discusses the theories of micro sociology such as choice
theory and symbolic interactionism. Cooley and Mead's works on
socialization and the development of the self are explained. The
importance of attachments is introduced and discussed in this
chapter. (This theme will be developed throughout the text.)
The chapter then discusses research, with emphasis on the
importance of ascertaining causation. Techniques for determining
causation are described. Ofshe's experimental study of
attachments and conformity is highlighted as the "over-the-
shoulder" example. Stark's study with Lofland on attachments and
conversion is keynoted as an example of nonexperimental research.
A discussion of replication concludes the chapter.

Capsule Summary

Theories are statements of how and why concepts are related. As
with concepts, theories are abstractions. Theories must be
subject to empirical verification. A theory may be proved false,
but no amount of research can completely prove a theory true.
Science consists of constructing and testing theories.
        Choice theory and symbolic interaction are examples of micro
theories in sociology. Micro theories assume that people make
choices based on rewards and costs. Choice theories assume that
since rewards are typically obtained from others, people engage in
exchange relationships and over time tend to establish stable
exchange partnerships with others. Attachments emerge from such
relationships, and norms function to ensure some basis for
predictability. Symbolic interaction focuses on the importance
of symbols, which stand for or indicate other things. Symbols
are essential for human communication. Cooley and Mead, founders
of symbolic interaction, focused on the processes of socialization
and the development of the self.
        Research is the process of making systematic observations.
Much research focuses upon testing specific hypotheses--testable
statements derived from theories. Research tries to establish
causation by establishing the presence of the three criteria of
causation: correlation, time order, and nonspuriousness.
Correlation can be established if it can be shown that two things
vary or change in unison. Time order can be demonstrated if it
can be shown that the cause (often termed the independent
variable) precedes the effect (often termed the dependent
variable). Nonspuriousness can be established if it can be
shown that the effect was not produced by something else.
Typically research studies are replicated by others to determine

whether or not the same results are consistently obtained.

Sociological research may be either <u>experimental</u> or <u>nonexperimental</u>. Nonexperimental research is probably more common since many of the problems typically studied by sociologists do not lend themselves well to laboratory research. Experiments offer greater control over the subjects. Nonexperimental research findings are more subject to risk. <u>Ofshe's</u> study of <u>attachments</u> and <u>conformity</u> is an example of experimental research. He was able to demonstrate <u>causation</u> by establishing the three criteria. He utilized <u>controls</u> and <u>randomization</u> to rule out the possibility of <u>spuriousness</u> and employed a <u>test of significance</u> to rule out chance. <u>Stark and Lofland's</u> study of attachments and conversion is an interesting example of nonexperimental research. They too were able to establish <u>correlation</u> and <u>time order</u> but, as is often the case with <u>observational studies</u>, <u>nonspuriousness</u> was more difficult to ascertain.

Key Concepts

You should be able to explain the following concepts. You should also be able to cite several examples of each concept.

Theory	62	Attachment	71
Micro sociology	64	Hypothesis	73
Choice premise	64	Causation	73
Reward	64	Correlation (positive and	
Cost	65	negative)	73
Exchange relations	66	Nonspuriousness	74
Goods	67	Variable	76
Interaction	67	Independent variable	76
Altruism	67	Dependent variable	77
Symbol	67	Experimental control	77
Self	69	Randomization	77
Socialization	69	Test of significance	77
Looking glass self	69	Nonexperimental research	79
Mind (G.H. Mead)	69	Field observation research	79
Taking the role of the other	70	Replication	82

Key Research Studies

You should be familiar with both the methodology and the results of the research studies cited here.

Ofshe: study of attachments and conformity among college students (experimental study) 75

Stark and Lofland: nonexperimental research on conformity and conversion 79

Be prepared to explain the assumptions of these theories and, when applicable, to cite related research findings.

>Micro sociology theories (in general)
>Choice theories
>Symbolic interactionism
>Looking glass self

Key Figures

You should be able to associate each person with his contribution and explain any concepts or theories associated with him.

>Charles H. Cooley: co-founder of symbolic interactionism; looking glass self; socialization and development of the self
>George Herbert Mead: co-founder of symbolic interactionism; taking the role of the other; mind and self

Completion

1. _____ are statements of how and why several concepts are related.

2. A theory must _____ and _____ certain events or conditions that can be checked.

3. Although it is possible to prove a theory to be _____, no amount of research can prove a theory to be _____.

4. Social science proceeds on the principle that, given our options and preferences, we choose to do that which we can expect to be most _____.

5. Psychologists believe behavior is shaped by _____.

6. Humans seek what they perceive to be _____ and avoid what they perceive to be _____.

7. Unselfish behavior to benefit others is termed _____.

8. _____ is the process by which we influence one another.

9. _____ are things that stand for or indicate other things and are of primary importance to the theory of _____.

10. Both Cooley and Mead concluded that each person's sense of self is _____.

11. Mead used the concept of _____ to identify understanding of symbols and the concepts of _____ to identify our learned understanding of the responses of others.

12. Mead termed the ability to put ourselves in another's place the ability to _____.

13. Over time people tend to establish stable _____ partnerships.

14. A stable and persistent pattern of interaction between two people is termed a(n) _____.

15. _____ is the process of making systematic observations.

16. _____ are specific predictions about the empirical or observable world.

17. The three criteria of causation are _____, _____, and _____.

18. The independent variable is used to indicate a(n) _____ while the dependent variable is used to indicate a(n) _____.

19. Ofshe found a significant correlation between _____ and conformity among students.

20. Stark and Lofland's study of _____ and conversion is an example of _____ research.

Multiple Choice

1. Theories:
   a. must predict and prohibit certain events or conditions that can be checked
   b. are abstract in that the explanations they provide apply to a wide range of phenomena
   c. can never be proven true
   d. a and b
   e. all of the above

2. Researchers contribute to scientific progress:
   a. by seeking evidence that will support theories
   b. by providing evidence that will prove a theory true
   c. by doing their utmost to disprove a theory
   d. a and b
   e. none of the above

3. Micro sociology departs from the other micro social science theories in that micro sociology:
   a. expands the concepts of reward and cost
   b. recognizes that much of what we want can only be gotten from others
   c. defines goods as the whole range of rewards that people seek
   d. a and b
   e. all of the above

4. Micro sociology consists primarily of the study of:
   a. individuals
   b. face-to-face interaction in small groups
   c. explaining the regularities and patterns that arise out of interaction and exchanges
   d. b and c
   e. none of the above

5. Symbols:
   a. are things that stand for or indicate other things
   b. are important for human communication
   c. are part of our genetic makeup
   d. a and b
   e. all of the above

6. The looking glass self is associated with:
   a. Charles H. Cooley
   b. George H. Mead
   c. Richard Ofshe
   d. John Lofland
   e. George Homans

7. Mead considered the mind to be:
   a. our learned understanding of the responses of others to our conduct
   b. our understanding of symbols
   c. an innate component of the brain
   d. all of the above
   e. none of the above

8. Mead argued that a child cannot take an effective part in most games until he or she:
   a. can take the role of the other
   b. has developed a superego
   c. has developed a sense of self
   d. a and c
   e. all of the above

9. Stable exchange partnerships:
   a. are of special importance to us
   b. are restricted to goods and services
   c. often lead to the forming of attachments
   d. a and c
   e. all of the above

10. Specific predictions about the empirical or observable world
     are termed:
     a. theories
     b. variables
     c. controls
     d. hypotheses
     e. norms

11. Criteria for establishing causality include:
     a. replication, time order, and correlation
     b. correlation, time order, and spuriousness
     c. correlation, nonspuriousness, and time order
     d. correlation, spuriousness, and time order
     e. correlation, time order, and replication

12. _____ occurs when two factors appear correlated with
     one seeming to cause the other when, in reality, the
     correlation is caused by a third, unnoticed factor.
     a. Nonspuriousness
     b. Spuriousness
     c. A negative correlation
     d. An inverse correlation
     e. none of the above

13. A positive correlation exists when:
     a. both factors decline
     b. both factors increase
     c. one factor rises while the other declines
     d. no relationship exists between the factors
     e. a and b

14. The term _____ variable is used to indicate a cause.
     a. dependent
     b. independent
     c. intervening
     d. spurious
     e. none of the above

15. To determine the criteria of nonspuriousness, Ofshe used:
     a. replication
     b. randomization
     c. controls
     d. b and c
     e. all of the above

16. In determining significance, both _____ and _____
     are taken into account.
     a. number of subjects, size of the correlation
     b. number of subjects, time order of the experiment
     c. size of the correlation, time order of the experiment
     d. number of subjects, ages of the subjects
     e. none of the above

17. Stark and Lofland's study is an example of _____.
    a. field observation research
    b. the experimental method
    c. replication research
    d. secondary research
    e. all of the above

18. Stark and Lofland concluded that the primary basis for conversion to the Unification Church was:
    a. ideology
    b. brainwashing
    c. social class membership
    d. attachments
    e. a and b

19. Replication studies of religious conversion have found:
    a. it is impossible to replicate nonexperimental research
    b. little support for the findings of Stark and Lofland's earlier study
    c. that ideology rather than attachments plays the major role in determining conversion
    d. that attachments play the major role in determining conversion
    e. b and c

20. _____ is the most common form of symbolic interaction.
    a. Gesture
    b. Conversation
    c. Body language
    d. Reading
    e. Writing

Essay

1. A. Name the three criteria of causation. (knowledge)
   B. Explain the three criteria of causation. (comprehension)
   C. Show how Ofshe was able to determine causation in his experiment. (analysis)

2. A. Define experimental and nonexperimental research. (knowledge)
   B. Design a study using either experimental or nonexperimental research. (application)
   C. Using examples from the text compare and contrast experimental and nonexperimental research. (analysis)

3. Distinguish between a theory and a hypothesis. Explain the following statement: "Researchers do not contribute to scientific progress by seeking evidence that will support theories but by doing their utmost to disprove them."

4. The premise that people make choices is central to micro theories in social science. Explain how this premise is incorporated by micro sociology.

5. Briefly explain symbolic interaction. Explain the theories of Cooley and Mead on the development of the self.

Answers

Completion

1. Theories
2. predict, prohibit
3. false, true
4. rewarding
5. reinforcement
6. rewards, costs
7. altruism
8. Social interaction
9. Symbols, symbolic interactionism
10. socially created
11. mind, self
12. take the role of the other
13. exchange
14. attachment
15. Research
16. Hypotheses
17. correlation, time order, nonspuriousness
18. cause, effect
19. attachments
20. attachments, nonexperimental

Multiple Choice

1. e
2. c
3. e
4. d
5. d
6. a
7. b
8. d
9. d
10. d
11. c
12. b
13. e
14. b
15. d
16. a
17. a
18. d
19. d
20. b

CHAPTER 4
Macro Sociology:
Structures and Systems

Overview

This chapter opens with examples of research on bystander apathy
and the relationship between religion and delinquency that
illustrate the relationship between micro and macro sociology.
The importance of attachments (a major theme of this text) is
again emphasized. Chapter 4 then describes survey research and
continues with a discussion of the elements of systems and the
subject matter of macro sociology. This chapter discusses in
depth the three theories of macro sociology: functionalism,
social evolution, and conflict. It closes with an "over-the-
shoulder" view of Paige's cross-cultural study of family
structures and political conflict. Following this chapter is a
special topic devoted to sampling.

Capsule Summary

Macro sociology is concerned with the study of social structures:
groups, institutions, organizations, and societies. Micro and
macro sociology are related, and often research in one area may
overlap into the other. In their studies of delinquency and
religious commitment, for example, Hirschi and Stark and others
began by examining areas typically associated with micro
sociology only to discover it was necessary instead to focus on
areas in macro sociology.
    Theories of macro sociology attempt to explain the existence
of social structures and their origins, differences, and
interrelationships, as well as the interplay between the
individual and the social structure. Macro sociology views
societies as social systems characterized by separate structures,
interdependency, and equilibrium. Macro sociology often studies
institutions and classes. Institutions are "clusters of roles,
groups, organizations, customs, and activities that meet the
basic needs of a society." Every society has at least five basic
institutions: the family, the economy, religion, the political
order, and education. Classes are groups of people who share a
similar position in a society's stratification system. Macro
sociology thus focuses on institutions and classes not only as
separate structures but also as interrelated parts striving
toward equilibrium.
    Macro sociological theories include functionalism, social
evolution, and conflict theory. Each of these focuses on social
structures yet each emphasizes different aspects of these
structures and makes different assumptions about them.
    Functionalism is concerned with functions or the part that
each element of the system contributes to the whole. Functional

theories have three components; they identify and explain an aspect of the system, that aspect's existence in terms of how it preserves another part from disruption, and the source of potential disruption. <u>Functionalism</u> also focuses on <u>functional alternatives</u> and <u>dysfunctions</u>.

<u>Social evolution</u> theory focuses on the <u>development of social structures</u> over time and how they <u>adapt</u> to their <u>physical</u> and <u>social environment</u>. It postulates that those societies that have developed structures best adapted to their circumstances tended to grow and become more powerful and complex. It focuses on all societies and does not make value judgments regarding the direction of change.

<u>Conflict theory</u> considers <u>conflicts within a structure</u> that arise from the <u>differing interests of competitive groups</u>. It emphasizes how the structure may be shaped by the interests of these groups, especially the more <u>powerful</u> ones who serve their needs at the expense of the less powerful. <u>Marx</u> argued that the social structures are created by the <u>ruling class</u>. <u>Weber</u> expanded the concept and emphasized the importance of <u>status groups</u>.

<u>Macro sociology</u> often uses <u>survey research</u>. <u>Samples</u> are drawn and <u>questionnaires</u> or <u>interviews</u> are administered. Attention is paid to ensuring that the criteria of causality are met. (Both the studies of Paige and of Stark and others illustrate this.) While macro sociology typically focuses on groups, institutions, and organizations, occasionally whole societies are compared and contrasted. <u>Paige's</u> research on <u>kinship structure</u> and <u>political conflict</u> used such a cross-cultural comparison and is an example of research in <u>macro sociology</u>.

Key Concepts

Be prepared to explain the concepts listed here and to cite several examples of each concept.

Social structure	88	Nuclear family	97
Macro sociology	88	Extended family	97
Survey research	89	Functional alternative	98
Sample	89	Dysfunction	99
System	94	Social evolution	99
Institution	94	The ruling class	100
The five basic social institutions	94	Status group	100
		Kinship	102
Class	94	Patrilocal rule of residence	102
Stratification	94		
Equilibrium	96	Matrilocal rule of residence	102
Functionalism	97		

The following concepts are contained in Special Topic 1.

Census	106	Stratified random sample	108
Simple random sample	107	Census tract	108

37

Key Research Studies

You should be familiar with both the methodology and the results of the following research studies.

Darley and Latane: bystander apathy   86
Hirschi and Stark: delinquency and religious commitment   89
Stark and others: church membership, geographical area, and delinquency   90
Paige: comparative study of family systems of primitive societies   102

Key Theories

You should be able to explain the assumptions of the theories and, when applicable, cite related research findings.

Macro sociology theories (in general)
Functionalism
Social evolution
Conflict theory

Key Figures

Be able to associate each person with his contribution and explain any concepts or theories associated with him.

Karl Marx: conflict theory; the ruling class
Max Weber: status group
Gerhard Lenski: social evolution

Completion

1. The results of the research by Darley and Latane found the larger the group believed to be present, the _____ an individual will feel personal responsibility to act in an emergency.

2. In survey research the data are collected by _____ or _____.

3. A relationship is _____ if it disappears when some third variable is controlled.

4. Macro sociological theories attempt to explain the existence of _____.

5. Macro sociologists assume societies are _____.

6. Because the parts of a system are interdependent they tend to fall into some kind of _____ or balance.

7. The five basic institutions in any society include the family, the economy, _____, _____, and _____.

8. _____ are clusters of specialized roles, groups, organizations, customs, and activities devoted to meeting social _____.

9. One adult couple and their children constitute a(n) _____ family.

10. Another structure by which the same function can be accomplished is termed a(n) _____.

11. Arrangements among structures that harm or distort the system are termed _____.

12. _____ theories suggest that societies with structures that enable them to adapt to their physical and social environments have a better chance for survival than do societies that fail to develop such structures.

13. A faulty assumption made by nineteenth-century social evolutionists was that social change is inevitable and _____.

14. _____ theorists ask how social structure serves the interests of various competing groups within a society.

15. An ethnic group is a good example of a(n) _____ group.

16. In cultures that possess a(n) _____ rule of residence, newlyweds reside near or with the bride's family.

17. Paige's research demonstrated a very strong correlation between _____ and political conflict.

Note: The following three questions are drawn from Special Topic 1.

18. A(n) _____ gathers information from every person in the population.

19. The odds that a sample will be like a whole population depend only on the _____ of the sample.

20. Sampling that proceeds through a series of levels is termed _____ sampling.

1. Research by Darley and Latane found that:
    a. the larger the group present, the more an individual will feel personal responsibility to act in an emergency
    b. the larger the group present, the less an individual will feel personal responsibility to act in an emergency
    c. the size of the group present has no effect on bystander apathy
    d. church attendance and delinquency rates are inversely correlated
    e. none of the above

2. Survey research:
    a. collects data using questionnaires and personal interviews
    b. utilizes samples
    c. can establish time order more easily than experiments can
    d. a and b
    e. all of the above

3. When sex differences were controlled, Hirschi and Stark found that:
    a. boys who attend church are less likely to be delinquents than are boys who do not attend church
    b. girls who attend church are less likely to be delinquents than are girls who do not attend church
    c. the more people present at an emergency, the more likely the victim is to receive help
    d. a and b
    e. none of the above

4. Research on delinquency and religion has found that:
    a. religion is negatively correlated with delinquency in schools where the majority of the students are religious
    b. religion is positively correlated with delinquency in schools where the majority of the students are religious
    c. religion is negatively correlated with delinquency in schools where most students are not religious
    d. religion is positively correlated with delinquency in schools where most students are not religious
    e. no correlation exists between religion and delinquency in schools where most of the students are religious

5. Elements of systems include:
    a. separate parts or structures
    b. interdependence among parts
    c. equilibrium among the parts
    d. b and c
    e. all of the above

6. Basic institutions found in all societies include:
   a. the family
   b. the political order
   c. religion
   d. a and c
   e. all of the above

7. Macro sociologists assume that:
   a. societies are never wholly static
   b. every structure is related to every other structure
   c. the same degree of interdependence among structures
      exists in all societies
   d. b and c
   e. all of the above

8. _____ theories explain social structures on the basis
   of their consequences for other parts of the system.
   a. Conflict
   b. Functional
   c. Social evolution
   d. Symbolic interaction
   e. Choice

9. Arrangements among structures that harm or distort the
   system are termed _____.
   a. functional alternatives
   b. functional requisites
   c. dysfunctions
   d. latent functions
   e. manifest functions

10. Contemporary evolutionary theories:
    a. always assume that all societies evolve to more complex
       cultures
    b. are meant to apply to specific cases
    c. assume that all change is inevitable and progressive
    d. all of the above
    e. none of the above

11. _____ theorists ask how social structure serves the
    interests of various competing groups within a society.
    a. Functional
    b. Conflict
    c. Social evolutionary
    d. Micro
    e. Choice

12. The term status group is most closely associated with:
    a. Marx
    b. Weber
    c. Lenski
    d. Paige
    e. Darley

13. Macro sociological research must always be based on:
    a. individuals
    b. the comparative study of groups
    c. case studies
    d. primitive societies
    e. none of the above

14. Societies with factional politics:
    a. reach decisions through competition and conflict
    b. stress agreement rather than disagreement
    c. contain internal groups that stress their own interests
    d. a and c
    e. none of the above

15. When Paige examined primitive societies, he found that:
    a. kinship and residence are primary bases for group formation
    b. conflict occurs primarily among men of different kinship groups
    c. patrilocal societies were often more communal than matrilocal societies
    d. a and b
    e. all of the above

16. Societies in which the bride leaves home after marriage and the couple takes up residence with or close to the husband's family have a _____ rule of residence.
    a. matrilocal
    b. neolocal
    c. patrilocal
    d. fratralocal
    e. nuclear

17. Paige's study of structure and conflict used _____.
    a. field research
    b. the experimental method
    c. comparative research
    d. simple random samples
    e. none of the above

Note: Questions 18 and 19 are drawn from the special topic on sampling.

18. If a person gathers information from every member of a population, he or she is conducting:
    a. a census
    b. a random sample
    c. a stratified random sample
    d. a random census
    e. cross-cultural research

19. The odds that a sample will be like the whole population depend on:
    a. the absolute size of the sample
    b. the ratio of the sample size to the population size
    c. the use of stratified rather than simple random samples
    d. a and b
    e. all of the above

20. Which of the following is/are not correctly paired with his or her contribution?
    a. Darley and Latane: bystander apathy
    b. Karl Marx: social evolutionary theory
    c. Max Weber: status group
    d. Paige: comparative study of family systems of primitive societies
    e. b and c

Essay

1. A. Explain functional and conflict theories. (comprehension)
   B. Attempt to integrate functional and conflict theories into a more general explanation of society. (application)
   C. Compare and contrast functional and conflict theories. (analysis)

2. A. Define micro and macro sociology. (knowledge)
   B. Explain the relationship between micro and macro sociology. (comprehension)
   C. Show how the research on religion and delinquency illustrates this relationship. (application)

3. Briefly discuss the research findings of Stark and others on religion and delinquency.

4. Using examples, discuss the three elements of a system.

5. Discuss Paige's research on kinship structure and political conflict.

Answers

Completion

1. less
2. personal interview, questionnaire
3. spurious
4. social structures
5. systems
6. equilibrium
7. religion, education, the political order
8. Institutions, needs
9. nuclear
10. functional alternative
11. dysfunctions
12. Social evolutionary
13. progressive
14. Conflict
15. status
16. matrilocal
17. rules of residence
18. census
19. absolute size
20. stratified random

Multiple Choice

1. b
2. d
3. e
4. e
5. e
6. e
7. a
8. b
9. b
10. e
11. b
12. b
13. b
14. d
15. d
16. c
17. c
18. a
19. a
20. b

CHAPTERS 1 TO 4
Review and Special Project

Review

Chapters 1 through 4 have introduced sociology, discussing it as a science and introducing many new concepts central to sociology. They have discussed both micro and macro sociology and the theory and research in these areas.

You may wish to test your knowledge of this material by actually trying your hand at doing some sociology. Although it might be difficult to conduct a study in a few weeks without administrative and financial backing, it is possible to design one. Through this design you will test your knowledge of several areas and obtain firsthand knowledge of sociology in action.

Special Project

Using students on your campus as subjects, assume you want to replicate one of the following studies: Ofshe's study of attachments and conformity, Milgram's "small world" research, or one of the studies on religion and delinquency conducted by Stark and others. Design a study based on the original study you have chosen.

As you design your study, be certain to address the following questions:

1. What did the original researcher hypothesize and what were his results?
2. What do you hypothesize? Do you expect similar results?
3. Is your research experimental or nonexperimental?
4. How will you draw your sample? What kind will you use?
5. What method will you use to gather your data?
6. How will you establish the criteria of causation?
7. Is your study more in the realm of micro or macro sociology?
8. Does your study use the assumptions of any particular theory? What are they?
9. Can you identify any problems or issues that might arise if you actually were to conduct this study? How might you address them in advance?

CHAPTER 5
Biology, Culture, and Society

Overview

Chapter 5 starts with a brief historical discussion of
instinctual and environmental theories of behavior. It explains
behavioral genetics and shows how most social scientists today
take a balanced position between heredity and environment.
Research such as the numerous studies of twins is cited to
support the notion of interplay between biology and environment.
After intelligence testing is discussed, the issue of race and
intelligence is raised with a brief summary of Jensen's
controversy. The chapter concludes with a discussion of research
findings from ethology and sociobiology on learned behavior among
animals and symbolic communication with primates.

Capsule Summary

Early in this century <u>instinctual theories</u> dominated the social
sciences. They postulated that behavior was inborn and the
result of <u>heredity</u>. By the 1930s, however, <u>environmental
theories</u> dominated. They postulated that behavior was strictly
the result of <u>cultural</u> and <u>social</u> influences with <u>biology</u> playing
no role.
 Today most social scientists assume that human behavior is
the result of the interplay between <u>biology</u> and <u>social</u> and
<u>cultural</u> environment. (The concepts <u>genotype</u> and <u>phenotype</u>
illustrate this interplay.) Indeed, the rapidly growing field of
<u>behavioral genetics</u> seeks to identify <u>traits</u> that <u>influence
behavior</u> and have some <u>genetic basis</u>. Research in this area has
emphasized the study of <u>identical twins</u>, particularly identical
twins <u>reared apart</u>. These twins often exhibit <u>similar although
not identical characteristics</u>. The interplay of heredity and
environment is illustrated by the research of <u>Tanner</u> and others
on the <u>increasing physical size</u> and the <u>decline</u> in the <u>age of the
onset of puberty</u> of Europeans and Americans over the past
century. They found that <u>environmental conditions</u> can suppress
<u>genetic potential</u>.
 <u>Intelligence testing</u> began with <u>Binet</u>, who developed what
was to become the <u>Stanford-Binet Test of Intelligence</u>. This test
and others compare a person's <u>mental age</u> with his or her <u>calendar
age</u> to determine an <u>intelligence quotient</u>. IQ test scores have
proven to be powerful predictors of academic or career success
and tend to vary little over a person's life. <u>IQ</u> testing came
under criticism, particularly when <u>Jensen</u> published a highly
controversial article, which argued that the differences between
the <u>scores</u> of <u>blacks</u> and <u>whites</u> were the result of <u>genetic</u>
differences. <u>Sowell</u>, in an ingenious study, determined that the
differences were due instead to <u>environmental</u> and <u>cultural</u>

suppression of innate potential, thus illustrating again the interplay between heredity and environment.

Sociologists have long assumed that humans differ from other animals in that we alone possess culture and language. Recent studies in ethology and sociobiology, however, have discovered evidence of learned behavior, tool making, and use of symbolic communication among other animals, particularly primates. The Harlows' research with monkeys showed that early isolation had detrimental effects on adult behavior such as sexual performance and social relationships. A landmark in the study of communication was reached when the Gardiners taught a chimp, Washoe, American sign language. Washoe was able to communicate through sign language and eventually to teach these signs to another infant chimp placed in her care.

Key Concepts

You should be prepared to explain the concepts and terms listed here, as well as give several examples of each concept.

Instinct	112	Intelligence quotient (IQ)	124
Chromosome	115	Language	129
Gene	115	Ethologist	129
Genotype	116	Sociobiology	134
Phenotype	116		

Key Research Studies

You should be familiar with both the methodology and the results of these research studies.

Rosenthal, Schuckit, and others: studies of twins 117
Tanner: declining age of the onset of puberty 121
Jensen: controversial study of race and IQ 125
Sowell: response to Jensen, race, IQ, and immigrant status 126
Harlow and Harlow: effects of isolation on infant monkeys 130
Gardiner and Gardiner: teaching American sign language to chimps 131

Key Theories

You should be able to explain the assumptions of these theories and, when applicable, cite related research findings.

Instinctual theory
Environmental theory
Behavioral genetics

Be able to associate each of the following with his or her contribution and explain any concepts or theories associated with him or her.

> William McDougall: social psychologist who proposed
> instinctual theory
>
> Alfred Binet: Stanford-Binet Test of Intelligence
> Jane Goodall: study of wild chimps
> Washoe: first chimp to learn American sign language

Completion

1. A(n) _____ is a form of behavior that occurs in all normal members of a species without having been learned.

2. The major proponent of instinctual theories was the social psychologist _____.

3. By the 1930s the social sciences were dominated by purely _____ theories.

4. Today we take the position that human beings are the result of the interplay between their _____ and their _____.

5. In our chromosomes are tiny structures termed _____ that contain DNA.

6. The _____ is the actual outcome of the interplay between the genotype and the environment.

7. Tanner found that the age of the onset of menstruation has _____ in Europe and the United States over the past century.

8. Intelligence testing was begun by the French psychologist _____.

9. An intelligence quotient is a person's _____ age divided by the calendar age multiplied by 100.

10. It has been found that IQ test scores are powerful predictors of _____ and _____.

11. In 1969 Jensen argued that interracial differences in average IQ were the result of _____.

12. It is widely recognized that much nonhuman behavior is _____.

13. Older introductory texts have often argued that humans differ from other animals in that only humans possess _____ and _____.

14. Students of animal behavior are called _____.

15. _____ argued that lower IQ scores among blacks are the result of environmental suppression of innate potential.

16. The Harlows' study of monkeys found that many of the effects of early isolation seem _____.

17. Altering or adapting natural materials in order to increase the ability to achieve some goal is termed _____.

18. The Gardiners taught Washoe to communicate through the use of _____.

19. Sociobiologists study the links between _____ and _____.

20. A virtue of animal studies is that we can manipulate the _____ to study adaptation.

Multiple Choice

1. Early instinctual theories:
   a. discounted the impact of cultural and social influences on human development
   b. dominated social science during the 1930s
   c. assigned no role to heredity
   d. b and c
   e. all of the above

2. The major proponent of instinctual theories was:
   a. Thomas Sowell
   b. Alfred Binet
   c. William McDougall
   d. James Tanner
   e. Arthur Jensen

3. Today most social scientists take the premise that human development results from:
   a. purely environmental influences
   b. purely biological influences
   c. an interplay between biology and environment
   d. purely cultural influences
   e. none of the above

4. The sum total of the genetic instructions that an organism receives from its parents is called the:
   a. genotype
   b. chromosomal number
   c. phenotype
   d. geno-number
   e. pheno-number

5. Behavioral geneticists have claimed considerable success in isolating human characteristics and behavior that are influenced to a substantial degree by genetic inheritance. Some of these include:
   a. alcoholism
   b. intelligence
   c. a tendency toward impulsive and aggressive behavior
   d. a and c
   e. all of the above

6. Studies of identical twins reared apart have found their IQs to be:
   a. identical
   b. extremely similar
   c. markedly different
   d. unmeasurable
   e. none of the above; no such subjects have been discovered

7. Social consequences of early maturation include:
   a. an increase in the age at marriage compared with the past century
   b. more permissive attitudes toward premarital sex
   c. a need for adult authority to be based on something other than size
   d. b and c
   e. all of the above

8. The recent increased acceptance of premarital sexual activity has resulted from:
   a. earlier sexual maturity
   b. more reliable methods of contraception
   c. legalized abortion
   d. b and c
   e. all of the above

9. Research has found that people in North America and Europe are _____ than they did in the past century.
   a. achieving puberty earlier
   b. growing and reaching their full size later
   c. marrying much later
   d. a and c
   e. all of the above

10. Intelligence testing was developed by:
    a. Arthur Jensen
    b. Alfred Binet
    c. Thomas Sowell
    d. John Stanford
    e. b and d

11. If a person's mental age is 25 percent higher than his or her calendar age, that person's IQ is:
    a. 100
    b. 125
    c. 75
    d. 115
    e. 150

12. IQ tests:
    a. have been found to be good indicators of school performance
    b. are very consistent over the person's life
    c. were seldom administered before 1950
    d. a and b
    e. all of the above

13. Jensen argued that the differences between the IQ scores of blacks and whites were the result of:
    a. environmental differences
    b. genetic differences
    c. environmental suppression of the genotype
    d. invalid testing instruments
    e. cultural deprivation

14. Sowell's research found that the differences in the IQ scores of blacks and whites were due to:
    a. genetic differences
    b. innate racial characteristics
    c. environmental suppression of innate potential
    d. a and b
    e. an invalid testing instrument

15. Sowell argued that IQ tests:
    a. were invalid when used on black children
    b. can reflect how social and cultural deprivation can damage people's abilities
    c. should be discontinued
    d. a and c
    e. none of the above

16. Ethologists study:
    a. primitive societies
    b. the interplay between environment and biology in humans
    c. animal behavior
    d. genetic potential in humans
    e. none of the above

17. The Harlows found that monkeys reared in total isolation:
    a. were no different from monkeys reared with other monkeys
    b. made up for early deficits when they joined monkey colonies
    c. were unable to engage in social and sexual relationships
    d. a and b
    e. none of the above

18. Sociobiologists might include:
    a. psychologists
    b. anthropologists
    c. sociologists
    d. b and c
    e. all of the above

19. Primate studies have advantages in that:
    a. we can manipulate the environment to study adaptation
    b. we can observe primates as substitutes for our most ancient ancestors
    c. we can seek basic elements of social organization by examining societies that have not been overlaid with a great deal of culture
    d. all of the above
    e. none of the above

20. The case of Washoe illustrates that:
    a. chimp behavior is determined entirely by instincts
    b. chimps can learn sign language but cannot use it to form sentences
    c. chimps cannot transmit language to their young
    d. chimps can learn to speak words
    e. none of the above

_____

Essay

1. A. Distinguish between genotypes and phenotypes. (knowledge)
   B. Explain the following statement: "Human beings are a result of the interplay between their biology and their social and cultural environment." (comprehension)
   C. Give an example of a human behavior or characteristic and show how it is the result of the interrelationship between genetic inheritance and the environment. (application)

2. A. Explain instinctual and environmental theories. (comprehension)
   B. Using current research, interrelate the role of heredity and environment. (application)
   C. Contrast instinctual and environmental theories. (analysis)

3. Discuss the race and IQ controversy. Show how Jensen's argument was countered by Sowell's research findings.

4. Show how Tanner's research illustrates the interplay between biology and environment.

5. Using the research studies on primates, show how these research findings do not support the premise that humans alone possess culture and can communicate through a formal system.

Answers

Completion

1. Instinct
2. William McDougall
3. environmental
4. biology, social and cultural environment
5. genes
6. phenotype
7. declined
8. Alfred Binet
9. mental
10. school performance, occupational success
11. genetic differences
12. instinctual
13. cultural and language
14. ethologists
15. Thomas Sowell
16. irreversible
17. tool making
18. American sign language
19. biology, behavior
20. environment

Multiple Choice

1. a
2. c
3. c
4. c
5. e
6. b
7. d
8. e
9. a
10. b
11. b
12. d
13. b
14. c
15. b
16. c
17. c
18. e
19. d
20. e

CHAPTER 6
Socialization and Social Roles

Overview

This chapter introduces the process of socialization and describes
research findings on the effects of early isolation and
deprivation as evidence of the importance of this process.
Piaget's work on cognitive development is discussed in depth.
Brown and Bellugi's work on language acquisition is also included
in the discussion of cognitive structures. The relationship
between interaction and cognitive development with an emphasis on
the attachment-teaching hypothesis is discussed. Emotional
development, the emergence of the self, and personality
development are described. Chapter 6 then considers the theory of
cultural determinism, its assumptions, research findings, and
recent criticisms. Margaret Mead's famous works provide examples
of extreme cultural determinism. Differential socialization is
discussed, and Kohn's research in this area is highlighted as the
"over-the-shoulder" example. Goffman's stage analogy of
interaction is described with examples of its concepts. Following
the chapter is a special topic that describes the origins and
current status of differential socialization on the basis of
gender.

Capsule Summary

Socialization is the crucial learning process that allows us to
possess culture and participate in social relations. Feral
children are examples of extreme isolation and deprivation. Early
studies such as those by Skeels and Dye documented the importance
of interaction and contact during the early years.
     For many years psychology was dominated by the stimulus-
response (SR) theory of learning, which argued that behavior was a
response to external stimuli and that learning was a result of
reinforcement. Piaget took issue with the SR theory and argued
that the human mind develops and functions on the basis of
cognitive structures. Through extensive research he proposed the
existence of four stages of cognitive development: sensorimotor,
preoperational, concrete operational, and formal operational.
Children in these stages differ in their ability to comprehend
concepts and situations. Others who endorsed the concept of
cognitive structures include Brown and Bellugi, whose research on
language acquisition indicated that young children's speech often
seems to indicate a search for grammatical rules.
     Piaget has been criticized for ignoring the role of social
interaction in his work. Recent research has focused upon the
relationship between verbal interaction and language acquisition
(the attachment-teaching hypothesis), and this research has
yielded some surprising results.

An important aspect of the socialization process is the emergence of the self. Research by Bain, Flavell, and others has expanded upon earlier work by Piaget and Mead. Personality refers to the consistent pattern of thoughts, feelings, and actions displayed by an individual. Personality emphasizes both the similarities and differences among individuals.

Cultural determinism was a dominant theory in anthropology in the 1920s and 1930s. In its extreme form, cultural determinism argues that personality is totally shaped by culture and that child-rearing practices are critical in determining later personality characteristics. Mead's works on adolescence in Samoa and sex and temperament are classic examples of cultural determinism. These studies have recently come under criticism, and today most social scientists take the position that culture and early socialization are important in shaping personality but are not the only factors.

Since not all people in a society are expected to play identical roles, not all members of a society are socialized exactly the same. Differential socialization accounts for some of the differences among people. Kohn's study, for example, found that parents often socialize their children on the basis of the roles that they expect them to perform. These expectations often reflect the parents' own working conditions.

Erving Goffman studied interaction from the point of view that the world is a stage upon which we are all actors. He distinguished between role and role performance and used concepts such as props, front stage and backstage, and impression management in his analogy.

Differential socialization is possibly best illustrated in sex-role socialization. Although the sexes do differ biologically, these differences were a more important basis for the assignment of roles in primitive societies than they are at present. These early societies laid the foundation for differential socialization by gender that has become a part of our culture. Today we still socialize males and females differently; however, recent changes in the nature of jobs and the increased participation of women in the work force calls into question the need, rationality, and desirability of continued differential socialization on the basis of gender.

Key Concepts

You should be able to explain the following concepts. You should also be prepared to cite several examples of each concept.

Feral children   136
Socialization   137
Cognitive structure   141
Sensorimotor stage   142
Preoperational stage   142
Concrete operational
   stage   142
Formal operational stage   142

Rule of object permanence
   142
Rule of conservation   142
Motherese   145
Self   145
Personality   146
Cultural determinism   147

Key Research Studies

You should be familiar with both the methodology and the results
of these research studies.

Key Figures

Be able to associate each person with his or her contribution.

    Erving Goffman: role performance, studied nonobservance, and
                impression management
    Jean Piaget: theory of cognitive stages
    Franz Boas: anthropologist; theory of cultural determinism
    Margaret Mead: anthropologist; theory of cultural determinism

Key Theories

You should be able to explain the assumptions of these theories
and, when applicable, to cite related research findings.

    Stimulus-response
    Theory of cognitive stages
    Cultural determinism

Completion

1. Children who are neglected and isolated from human contact are termed _____.

2. The learning process by which infants become normal human beings, possessing culture and able to participate in social relations, is termed _____.

3. Socialization related to roles and to role expectations is called _____ socialization.

4. The theory that behavior is merely a response to external stimuli and that we repeat whatever behavior has been reinforced by our environment is termed _____.

5. Piaget argued that the human mind develops and functions on the basis of _____ or general rules for reasoning.

6. Piaget's cognitive stages include the sensorimotor, _____, concrete operational, and _____.

7. The rule of _____ is Piaget's term for the principle that objects continue to exist even when they are out of sight.

8. The final stage in Piaget's theory of cognitive development is the _____.

9. Researchers have concluded that perhaps _____ of all adults do not reach the formal operations stage.

10. Brown and Bellugi found that young children experiment with speech in ways that appear to involve a search for _____.

11. An individual's consistent pattern of thoughts, feelings, and actions are termed his or her _____.

12. _____ published and taught the theory of cultural determinism.

13. Mead described the _____ as gentle, unaggressive, and passive and argued that both men and women have "feminine temperaments."

14. _____ wrote both <u>Coming of Age in Samoa</u> and <u>Sex and Temperament in Three Primitive Societies</u>.

15. Kohn found that _____ experienced by parents influenced whether they stressed conformity or self-expression rearing their children.

16. Kohn found that in contrast to working-class parents, middle-class parents were more concerned about their children being capable of _____ and _____.

17. A study in which observations are made of the same people at several different times is termed a(n) _____ study.

18. The actual conduct of a particular individual while on duty in a position is called _____.

19. Goffman termed the conscious manipulation of role performance _____.

20. A set of norms attached to a position that, in turn, violates the norms adhered to by the larger society is termed a(n) _____.

Multiple Choice

1. The socialization process:
   a. is a learning process
   b. begins at birth and ends at death
   c. literally means to be "made social"
   d. a and c
   e. all of the above

2. Skeels and Dye found that orphan infants who had been placed under the personal care of an older girl showed _____ when compared with those who remained in the orphanage.
   a. slight improvement
   b. dramatic improvement
   c. no improvement
   d. slight decline in ability
   e. marked decline in ability

3. The stimulus-response theory postulated that learning results from:
   a. reinforcement
   b. cognitive structures
   c. developmental stages
   d. instincts
   e. heredity

4. The last stage of cognitive development is the:
   a. preoperational
   b. formal operational
   c. sensorimotor
   d. concrete operational
   e. sensorioperational

5. During the concrete operational stage, a child lacks:
   a. the rule of object permanence
   b. the rule of conservation
   c. the ability to take the role of the other
   d. all of the above
   e. none of the above

6. Researchers estimate that about _____ of all adults do
   not reach the formal operations stage.
   a. one-fourth
   b. one-third
   c. one-half
   d. two-thirds
   e. three-quarters

7. In their study of language acquisition, Brown and Bellugi
   discovered that:
   a. young children's speech contains only the most vital
      words
   b. parents frequently echo their children, thus expanding
      and correcting their sentences
   c. young children experiment with speech in ways that seem
      to involve a search for grammatical rules
   d. a and c
   e. all of the above

8. Research in the area of the attachment-teaching hypothesis
   has shown that:
   a. children who are exposed to motherese acquire language
      much more rapidly than those who are not
   b. children who are talked to learn to talk sooner and
      better than children who are not talked to
   c. the degree of attachments a child enjoys plays a major
      role in language acquisition
   d. all of the above
   e. none of the above

9. In terms of their personalities:
   a. all humans are alike in some ways
   b. all humans are like only some other humans
   c. all humans are unique in some ways
   d. b and c
   e. all of the above

10. The principle of cultural determinism argues that
    individuals' personalities:
    a. are tiny replicas of their cultures
    b. are the result of an interplay between biology and
       culture
    c. are totally the result of heredity
    d. are not well developed among primitive people
    e. none of the above

11. The theory of cultural determinism is most closely associated with:
    a. Jean Piaget
    b. Franz Boas
    c. Roger Brown
    d. Melvin Kohn
    e. Erving Goffman

12. Margaret Mead argued that the differences in temperament between the Arapesh and the Mundugumor were the result of:
    a. innate biological differences
    b. child-rearing practices, especially during infancy
    c. the physical location of their respective societies
    d. b and c
    e. none of the above

13. In his _initial_ study, Kohn found that middle-class parents typically stressed the value(s) of:
    a. self-expression
    b. independence
    c. conformity
    d. a and b
    e. all of the above

14. In his _later_ studies, Kohn found that parents differed in their child-rearing practices _primarily_ on the basis of the parents':
    a. social class
    b. work conditions
    c. educational level
    d. a and c
    e. none of the above

15. In a longitudinal study, observations are made of:
    a. different people at several different times
    b. different people at the same time
    c. the same people at several different times
    d. nonhuman animals in natural settings
    e. none of the above

16. Goffman defined _____ as "the conscious manipulation of scenery, props, costumes, and our behavior in order to convey a particular role image to others."
    a. role failure
    b. studied nonobservance
    c. impression management
    d. backstage behavior
    e. teamwork

17. When we pretend not to see miscues in others' role performance, we are practicing:
    a. role failure
    b. studied nonobservance
    c. impression management
    d. backstage behavior
    e. teamwork

18. Juhasz's study of self-esteem of seventh- and eighth-graders found that _____ has a potent effect on self-conceptions.
    a. gender
    b. academic abilities
    c. parental occupation
    d. religion
    e. none of the above

Note: The following two questions are drawn from Special Topic 2.

19. The socialization process of males and females differs during:
    a. infancy
    b. teens
    c. childhood
    d. all of the above
    e. none of the above

20. Richer's results suggest that:
    a. the younger children display gender preferences in their play but the older children don't
    b. young children do not display gender differences in their play
    c. the gender preferences of the slightly older children seem to be innate
    d. b and c
    e. none of the above

Essay

1. A. List Piaget's four stages of cognitive development. (knowledge)
   B. Describe these stages using examples. (comprehension)
   C. Contrast the type of thinking characteristic of a child in the preoperational stage with that of a child in the concrete operations stage. (analysis)

2. A. Explain the stimulus-response theory of learning. (knowledge)
   B. Show how the work of Piaget or of Brown and Bellugi does not support the assumptions of SR theory. (comprehension)
   C. Design a study to test Piaget's theory or replicate the work of Brown and Bellugi. (application)

3. Explain cultural determinism. Discuss Mead's studies as an example of extreme cultural determinism.

4. Discuss some of the recent criticisms of Mead's work. Explain the contemporary position held by most sociologists regarding the relationship between culture and personality.

5. Explain differential socialization. Discuss Kohn's work in this area.

Answers

Completion

1.	Feral children	11.	personality
2.	socialization	12.	Franz Boas
3.	differential	13.	Arapesh
4.	stimulus-response	14.	Margaret Mead
5.	cognitive structures	15.	work conditions
6.	preoperational, formal operational	16.	self-expression, independence
7.	object permanence	17.	longitudinal
8.	formal operational stage	18.	role performance
9.	one-half (50 percent)	19.	impression management
10.	grammatical rules	20.	deviant role

Multiple Choice

1.	e	11.	b
2.	b	12.	b
3.	a	13.	d
4.	b	14.	b
5.	e	15.	c
6.	c	16.	c
7.	e	17.	b
8.	b	18.	a
9.	e	19.	d
10.	a	20.	b

CHAPTER 7
Deviance and Conformity

Overview

Chapter 7 begins with an introduction to deviant behavior,
discussing both early and contemporary biological theories of
deviance and related research findings. Personality theory and
its relationship to aggressive behavior is then discussed as an
example of a psychological approach. Sociological theories are
introduced with a brief discussion of the importance of
attachments. The chapter then discusses in depth the major
sociological theories of deviance: differential
association/social learning, subcultural deviation, structural
strain, control, anomie, and labeling. In each case, the major
assumptions of the theory are considered, relevant research
findings are cited, and shortcomings and criticisms of the theory
are noted. In the discussion of control theory, Crutchfield and
Stark's study of crime rates and moral and social integration is
described as the "over-the-shoulder" example. Chapter 7 ends
with an attempt to combine key elements of all the major
sociological theories into a more general theory of deviance.

Capsule Summary

Behavior that violates norms is termed <u>deviant behavior</u>. Serious
deviance depends on both the <u>importance</u> of the norm that was
violated and the <u>frequency</u> of norm violation. Distinctions can be
made between <u>intentional</u> deviance, which involves <u>rational</u>
<u>calculation</u>, and <u>duration</u> and <u>impulsive</u> deviance, which <u>lacks</u>
these <u>criteria</u>.
     There are sociological and nonsociological theories of
deviation. <u>Biological</u> theories attempt to show how deviants
differ physically from nondeviants. <u>Lombroso's</u> theory of "born
criminals" and the more recent approach of <u>Gove</u> (<u>age, gender,</u>
<u>biology, and deviance</u>) are examples of biological explanations.
Similarly, most <u>psychological research</u> has been unable to find a
significant relationship between <u>personality</u> type and <u>deviance</u>
although recent studies do indicate a possible link between
<u>violent behavior</u> and <u>self-esteem</u>.
     <u>Sociological</u> theories of deviance include <u>differential</u>
<u>association/social learning</u>, <u>subcultural deviance</u>, <u>structural</u>
<u>strain</u>, <u>control</u>, <u>anomie</u>, and <u>labeling</u>. Each of these is based on
different assumptions and each has certain shortcomings.
     <u>Sutherland's</u> theory of <u>differential association</u> argues that
deviant behavior, like other behavior, is learned through
socialization. Thus, attachments to others who are deviant may
encourage deviation. Later learning theories have included the
concept of <u>selective reinforcement</u> to further explain this
process.

Subcultural deviance emphasizes the conflicts over norms, which may arise in a society that contains many subcultures. Thus, behavior that may be conforming in a deviant subculture may be deviant to the general culture.

Merton's theory of structural strain argues that deviance results from the frustrations experienced by those who occupy disadvantaged positions in the stratification system. It argues that in attempting to conform to culturally approved goals, the poor will find the legitimate means to these goals blocked and hence will resort to illegitimate deviant means to attain them.

Attempting to explain conformity rather than deviance, control theory argues that conformity is tied to the bonds between an individual and the group. If the bonds are strong, the individual is more likely to conform. It recognizes the existence of four types of bonds--attachments, involvements, investments, and beliefs--and argues that an individual is likely to deviate when these bonds are weak.

Anomie (literally "normlessness") argues that deviance is the result of low social and moral integration. This idea was first proposed by Durkheim in his discussion of moral communities. Recent studies by Crutchfield and Stark have found significant relationships between the degree of social and moral integration of an area and crimes that involve intentional deviance.

Labeling theory distinguishes between primary and secondary deviation and focuses on the effect that a deviant label has on both the recipient and the society. It argues that labels are not uniformly applied to all deviants and that ultimately the label itself may cause a return to deviant behavior.

Each of these theories contains elements useful in explaining deviance. Similarly, each has been criticized for its shortcomings. To construct a general theory of deviation, therefore, elements of all these theories should be integrated into a more complete explanation.

Key Concepts

You should be able to explain the concepts listed here. Be prepared to cite several examples of each concept.

Key Research Studies

Be familiar with both the methodology and the results of the following research studies.

Gove: age, gender, biology, and deviance 171
Berkowitz: relationship between aggressive behavior and self-
            esteem 173
Linden and Fillmore: delinquency study in Canada (combination
                    of differential association and control
                    theory) 183
Crutchfield: social integration and crime rates 186
Stark: moral integration and crime rates 187

Key Figures

You should be able to associate each person with his contribution.

Cesare Lombroso: father of modern criminology; "born
                criminals"
Edwin Sutherland: theory of differential association
Robert Burgess and Ronald Akers: social learning (refined
                                differential association)
Robert K. Merton: strain theory; relationship between
                cultural means and goals
Emile Durkheim: control theory; anomie

Key Theories

Know how to explain the assumptions of these theories and, when applicable, cite related research findings.

Biological theory of deviance
Personality (psychological) theory of deviance
Differential association (social learning)
Subcultural deviance
Structural strain
Control theory
Anomie
Labeling

Completion

1. Behavior that does not conform to norms is termed
    _____.

2. Serious deviance depends not only on the _____ of the norm violated but also on the _____ of norm violation.

3. The concept of "born criminals" is associated with _____.

4. Gove argued that physically demanding forms of deviant behavior are overwhelmingly committed by _____.

5. Berkowitz found a relationship between _____ and self-esteem.

6. Sutherland proposed the theory of _____, which argued that all behavior is the result of socialization by means of interaction.

7. _____ can be explained as conflicts over norms.

8. _____ theories attempt to explain deviance on the basis of frustration caused by a person's position in the social structure.

9. _____ argued that deviance is a built-in consequence of stratification.

10. The initial assumption made by all _____ theories is that life is a vast cafeteria of temptation.

11. For control theory, the causes of conformity are the _____ between an individual and the group.

12. Types of social bonds include attachments, investments, _____, and _____.

13. Anomie is a condition of _____.

14. Durkheim argued that moral communities are characterized by moral integration and _____.

15. Crutchfield's study focused upon the relationship between crime rates and _____.

16. _____ deviance involves rational calculation and duration.

17. Secondary deviance is a reaction to having been _____.

18. _____ deviance lacks calculation and duration.

19. Stark and others argue that sociological theories of deviance should apply only to instances of _____ deviance.

20. _____ deviance involves actions that cause others to label an individual as deviant.

1. Serious deviance depends on:
   a. the importance of the norm violated
   b. the age of the violator
   c. the frequency of norm violation
   d. a and c
   e. all of the above

2. Which of the following statements is/are true?
   a. Some actions are regarded as deviant only in some societies.
   b. In all societies some people commit acts of serious deviance.
   c. All societies punish their deviants.
   d. a and b
   e. all of the above

3. According to Lombroso's theory, violent criminals:
   a. differ biologically from noncriminals
   b. have low self-esteem
   c. are under age 30
   d. experience frustration caused by poverty
   e. learn crime in association with other criminals

4. Sutherland's theory of differential association attributed deviance to:
   a. biological differences between deviants and nondeviants
   b. low self-esteem
   c. strain or frustration caused by poverty
   d. being labeled deviant
   e. attachments to others who are deviant

5. Gove's research revealed that:
   a. the arrest rate for violent crimes is highest for ages 25-30
   b. females are more likely to be arrested for violent crimes than males are
   c. the arrest rate for violent crimes drops markedly after age 30
   d. a and c
   e. all of the above

6. Berkowitz found that men who commit violent acts such as assault:
   a. are biologically different from those who do not
   b. have low self-esteem
   c. are often members of deviant subcultures
   d. are very passive people who had suppressed their aggression too long
   e. none of the above

7. Differential association theory is most closely associated with:
   a. Cesare Lombroso
   b. Robert Merton
   c. Edwin Sutherland
   d. Emile Durkheim
   e. Leonard Berkowitz

8. Subcultural deviance:
   a. can be explained as conflicts over norms
   b. lets us understand that deviance is often a matter of definition
   c. explains deviation both among and within subcultural groups
   d. a and b
   e. all of the above

9. Which of the following men is/are not correctly matched with his theory?
   a. Sutherland: differential association
   b. Merton: subcultural deviance
   c. Durkheim: anomie
   d. Lombroso: born criminals
   e. b and c

10. Structural strain theory attempts to explain deviance as a response to:
    a. a deviant label that stigmatizes a person
    b. conflicts over norms
    c. a low rate of moral integration
    d. deviant attachments
    e. none of the above

11. Structural strain theory has been criticized because:
    a. studies have found that a person's social class is barely, if at all, related to committing crimes
    b. the theory seems to predict less deviance than actually occurs
    c. the theory offers no explanation for deviant behavior committed by wealthy people
    d. a and c
    e. all of the above

12. Bonds between the individual and the group include:
    a. attachments
    b. beliefs
    c. investments
    d. a and c
    e. all of the above

13. Control theory argues that deviant behavior is more likely to occur when:
    a. people have less to gain from deviance than from conformity
    b. an individual spends a good deal of time and effort on activities that conform to the norms
    c. the bonds between the individual and the group are weak
    d. a and b
    e. none of the above

14. The costs we have expended in constructing a satisfactory life and the current and potential flow of rewards coming to us are termed:
    a. investments
    b. involvements
    c. attachments
    d. beliefs
    e. none of the above

15. Linden and Fillmore's study of delinquency found that:
    a. attachments to parents and liking school were negatively correlated with being delinquent
    b. attachments to parent and liking school were positively correlated with having delinquent friends
    c. attachments to delinquent peers greatly increase the level of delinquency
    d. a and c
    e. b and c

16. According to Durkheim, moral communities are characterized by:
    a. low rates of moral integration
    b. high rates of anomie
    c. shared beliefs, especially religious beliefs
    d. b and c
    e. none of the above

17. Research by Crutchfield and Stark has found that moral and social integration:
    a. can inhibit impulsive deviance
    b. can limit intentional deviance
    c. can limit all types of crime
    d. do not affect crime rates
    e. none of the above

18. Mizruchi has suggested the term _____ as the best translation of _anomie_ into English.
    a. social disorganization
    b. deregulation
    c. moral disorganization
    d. role failure
    e. none of the above

19. Impulsive deviance:
    a. lacks calculation and duration
    b. involves rational calculation and duration
    c. can easily be explained by sociological theories
    d. a and c
    e. b and c

20. Deviant labels may incline persons toward further deviation because:
    a. a deviant label limits legitimate occupational opportunities
    b. being labeled may increase illegitimate economic opportunities
    c. a deviant label can affect self-conceptions
    d. a and b
    e. all of the above

_____
Essay

1. A. Explain the theories of differential association, subcultural deviance, and structural strain. (knowledge)
   B. Discuss two criticisms or shortcomings of each of these theories. (comprehension)
   C. Integrate these theories into a more complete explanation of deviance. Use an example. (analysis)

2. A. Explain the labeling theory. (knowledge)
   B. Discuss one criticism or shortcoming of this theory. (comprehension)
   C. Using a fictitious example, apply labeling theory to explain continued deviation. (application)

3. Discuss two biological theories of deviance. Show how research findings did or did not support these theories.

4. Discuss control theory. Be certain to explain in detail the four types of bonds that exist between the group and the individual.

5. Explain Durkheim's concepts of anomie and moral communities, and discuss two research findings about moral and social integration and crime rates.

_____
Answers

Completion

1. deviant behavior
2. importance, frequency
3. Cesare Lombroso
4. males
5. aggressive behavior
6. differential association
7. Subcultural deviance
8. Structural strain
9. Merton
10. control

11. social bonds
12. involvements, beliefs
13. normlessness
14. social integration
15. social integration
16. Intentional
17. labeled a deviant
18. Impulsive
19. intentional
20. Primary

Multiple Choice

1. d
2. e
3. a
4. e
5. c
6. b
7. c
8. d
9. b
10. e

11. d
12. e
13. b
14. a
15. d
16. c
17. b
18. b
19. a
20. e

CHAPTER 8
Social Control

Overview

A discussion of social control opens Chapter 8. It briefly
describes mechanisms of informal social control and highlights
the research by Asch and Schachter on the effects of the group on
the behavior of its members. It then discusses more formal
mechanisms of control and efforts of prevention, highlighting the
Cambridge-Somerville experiment on delinquency prevention. This
chapter also considers Gibbs's theory of deterrence, related
research findings, and efforts to reform and resocialize deviants,
including the TARP experiment. An appraisal of the current
effectiveness of informal and formal mechanisms of social control
closes the chapter.

Capsule Summary

Collective efforts to ensure conformity are forms of social
control. Most social control is informal and relies on our
internalization of the norms, attachments, and power of groups to
encourage conformity among their members. Laboratory studies
such as Asch's famous line experiments and Schachter's study of
group reactions to nonconformity have empirically demonstrated
the power of groups to affect the behavior of their members.
    When informal methods fail to produce conformity and the
deviance is also illegal or there are legal grounds for
intervention, more formal mechanisms such as police, prisons, and
mental hospitals are used. Formal controls are attempted in
three ways: to prevent deviance by removing opportunities for it
to occur, to deter deviance through the threat of punishment, and
to reform or resocialize deviants to discourage them from future
deviance.
    In order for a deviant act to occur, there must be an
opportunity to commit it. Hence many programs such as
neighborhood block watches seek to remove these opportunities.
It has long been assumed that delinquency has its roots in early
socialization. Numerous intervention programs such as the
Cambridge-Somerville experiment attempted to stem this tide;
however, such experiments failed to produce the desired results.
    Deterrence is based on the premise that the threat of
punishment will discourage deviation. Although this idea was
initially rejected by social scientists, recent studies such as
those conducted by Gibbs, Phillips, Sherman and Berk, and
Ehrlich indicate that the threat of punishment may deter
deviance provided the punishment is perceived of as swift,
certain, and severe. Indeed, the relative ineffectiveness of our
current criminal justice system in preventing deviance may stem
from the fact that these three criteria are not often met.

Much attention has recently been paid to the therapeutic function of prisons. Attempts have been made to resocialize and reform prisoners in the hope that they would not return to crime upon release. Again, studies such as the TARP experiment do not indicate any significant effect of these efforts, and recidivism rates remain high.

While recent data may seem pessimistic, social control is effective in many cases. Actually, few people commit crimes, but for those few who do engage in serious deviation, the current criminal justice system has not proven to be very effective.

Key Concepts

You should be able to explain the concepts listed here; be prepared to supply several examples of each concept.

Informal social control	198	Auburn prison model	217
Internalization of norms	198	Penitentiary	216
Formal social control	201	Recidivism	219
Deterrence	205	Resocialization	219

Key Research Studies

Know both the methodology and the results of the following research studies.

Asch: study of group conformity   199
Schachter: group reactions to nonconformity   200
Cabot and others: delinquency prevention by socialization
            (Cambridge-Somerville experiment)   202
Gibbs and others: effects of punishment on deterrence   209
Sherman and Berk: deterring wife beating   210
Ehrlich: capital punishment and deterrence   213
Lenihan, Rossi, and Berk: financial support of released
                  convicts and recidivism rates
                  (TARP study)   220

Key Theories

Although attempts at prison reform are not theories in the typical sense, they are broader than concepts and do make assumptions, so they are included here.

Opportunity theory
Deterrence theory
Attempts at prison reform

Completion

1. All collective efforts to ensure conformity to the norms are forms of _____.

2. When _____ methods of control fail and more serious acts of deviance occur, _____ methods of social control are activated.

3. Activities by organizations created to ensure conformity to the norms are termed _____.

4. When norms become _____, they become a part of our own beliefs about how we should act.

5. In his famous line experiments, Asch showed the influence of the group on _____.

6. Formal social control attempts to prevent deviance, to _____, and to reform or resocialize people.

7. Opportunity theory argues that in order for a crime to occur there must be people motivated to commit an offense, suitable targets, and a(n) _____.

8. The Cambridge-Somerville experiment found that the socialization program had _____ effect on delinquency.

9. The use of punishment to discourage people from deviance is termed _____.

10. Gibbs postulated that the more rapid, the more _____, and the more _____ the punishment for a crime, the lower the rate at which such a crime will occur.

11. It has been found that what matters is not the actual certainty, swiftness, or severity of punishment but the _____ of these aspects of punishment.

12. Sherman and Berk found that men who were arrested for wife beating were _____ likely to commit a new offense than those who were advised or ordered to leave.

13. Sherman and Berk's study of wife beating offered strong support for _____ theory.

14. Phillips argued that deterrence depends on how much _____ is given to executions.

15. According to Table 8-1, the least reported crime is _____.

16. About _____ as many crimes are committed as are reported.

17. In the 1800s and early 1900s most prisons were modeled after the _____ design.

18. The proportion of those released from prison who are sentenced to prison again is termed the _____.

19. Efforts to change a person's socialization--to socialize a person over again in hopes of getting him or her to conform to the norms--is called _____.

20. Whether capital punishment works and whether it is morally justified are _____ questions.

Multiple Choice

1. Formal social control is attempted through:
   a. preventing deviance
   b. deterring deviance
   c. reforming deviants
   d. a and b
   e. all of the above

2. Asch's experiments found that:
   a. a high proportion of people will conform even in a weak situation
   b. a low proportion of people will conform even in a weak situation
   c. the smaller the group, the greater the influence of the group on conformity
   d. the larger the group, the greater the influence of the group on conformity
   e. a and d

3. Schachter's study of group conformity found that:
   a. when the paid deviants stuck to their position, they began to receive less attention
   b. as soon as the paid deviants expressed their views, they began to receive less attention
   c. group members tended to like the deviant as well as they liked the more conforming members of the group
   d. all of the above
   e. none of the above

4. Formal social control is attempted by:
   a. preventing deviance
   b. deterring deviance by threat of punishment
   c. reforming people
   d. a and b
   e. all of the above

5. Opportunity theory recognizes that for a crime to occur, there must be:
   a. the presence of effective guardians
   b. suitable targets
   c. people motivated to commit an offense
   d. a and c
   e. b and c

6. The Cambridge-Somerville experiment found that:
   a. boys in the experimental group committed fewer delinquent acts than did boys in the control group
   b. boys in the experimental group committed more delinquent acts than did boys in the control group
   c. there was no difference in conviction rates between the experimental group and the control group
   d. the more publicity given an execution, the lower the homicide rate
   e. the smaller the group, the greater its influence on conformity

7. Experiments in the area of delinquency prevention have generally:
   a. been highly successful in preventing delinquency
   b. been failures in preventing delinquency
   c. succeeded in changing the circumstances of the children
   d. a and c
   e. none of the above

8. Gibbs postulated that the more _____ the punishment for a crime, the lower the rate at which such a crime will occur.
   a. severe
   b. certain
   c. swift
   d. a and c
   e. all of the above

9. Gibbs's theory of deterrence:
   a. predicts that severe sentences will not effectively deter crimes if people realize that they have little chance of being caught
   b. can apply to all deviant acts
   c. was not supported by empirical research
   d. a and c
   e. all of the above

10. In their study of wife beating, Sherman and Berk found that those men who had the highest rate of repeat offenses were those who had:
    a. been arrested
    b. been ordered to leave the premises
    c. been offered some advice and mediation
    d. been labeled deviant
    e. none of the above

11. The use of punishment to discourage people from committing deviance is termed:
    a. prevention
    b. deterrence
    c. resocialization
    d. revenge
    e. reform

12. Capital punishment has been opposed on:
    a. grounds of racial discrimination
    b. religious grounds
    c. results of research studies
    d. a and b
    e. all of the above

13. Phillips's study of capital punishment as deterrence found:
    a. no evidence that capital punishment deters homicide
    b. that the homicide rate is lower immediately following a well-publicized execution
    c. that the deterrent effect depends upon how much publicity is given to an execution
    d. b and c
    e. none of the above

14. Table 8-1 indicates that the most reported crime is:
    a. auto theft
    b. larceny
    c. rape
    d. purse snatching
    e. burglary

15. Table 8-2 indicates that the crime most likely to be solved is:
    a. assault
    b. rape
    c. robbery
    d. homicide
    e. a and b

16. Punishment for those who commit crimes in the United States is:
    a. very certain
    b. very swift
    c. very severe
    d. all of the above
    e. none of the above

17. The first to experiment with the use of a penitentiary were:
    a. the ancient Greeks under Plato
    b. the Quakers in Pennsylvania
    c. the British during the 1700s
    d. the researchers in Cabot's Cambridge-Somerville experiment
    e. none of the above

18. Reform efforts in prison are probably hampered by:
    a. a further weakening of an inmate's attachments with conventional people
    b. the stigma associated with being an ex-convict, which hinders the formation of attachments with conventional people
    c. new attachments to other deviants made while in prison
    d. a and b
    e. all of the above

19. In the TARP experiment, the recidivism rate for the control group was _____ the experimental group.
    a. much lower than
    b. much higher than
    c. slightly lower than
    d. slightly higher than
    e. the same as

20. Which of the following statements is/are true?
    a. If crime could be reduced by overhauling the criminal justice system, we could expect truly dramatic changes.
    b. A great deal of our conformity is rooted in informal social control.
    c. Social control does not appear to work because more than 13 million crimes are reported each year.
    d. all of the above
    e. none of the above

Essay

1. A. Name the three criteria that must be present if punishment is to serve as a deterrent. (Gibbs) (knowledge)
    B. Explain Gibbs's theory of deterrence. (comprehension)
    C. What does Gibbs's theory imply about our current criminal justice system? (application)

2. A. Describe either Asch's or Schachter's study of group conformity. (comprehension)
    B. Show how these results might effect real world (rather than laboratory) social interaction. (application)
    C. Compare and contrast these studies in terms of methodology and results. (analysis)

3. Discuss the Cambridge-Somerville experiment. What do the results of this and other intervention programs imply about delinquency prevention?

4. Discuss the capital punishment controversy by examining the issues involved and recent research findings.

5. Briefly trace the history of prisons in the United States. Explain why contemporary prisons, for the most part, fail in their mission to reform inmates.

Answers

Completion

1. social control
2. informal, formal
3. formal methods of social control
4. internalized
5. an individual's conformity
6. deter deviance
7. absence of effective guardians
8. no
9. deterrence
10. certain, severe
11. perceptions
12. less
13. deterrence
14. publicity
15. larceny
16. twice
17. Auburn
18. recidivism rate
19. resocialization
20. unrelated

Multiple Choice

1. e
2. a
3. a
4. e
5. e
6. c
7. b
8. e
9. a
10. c
11. b
12. e
13. d
14. a
15. d
16. e
17. b
18. e
19. e
20. b

CHAPTERS 5 TO 8
Review and Special Project

Review

This unit discussed the relationship between the individual and the group, as well as the biological and cultural basis for behavior. It emphasized informal and formal social control and described the various theories of deviation. You may wish to apply your knowledge of this material to the following project.

Special Project

Conduct an interview with someone who has committed an act that would qualify as a serious deviance. This need not be an illegal act; it could be behavior that, if discovered, would have resulted in trouble with the police, school authorities, or employers. The subject need not have been caught. It will probably not be difficult to locate such a person; remember that what may be conforming in one subculture may be deviant in the general culture.

Be certain to secure your subject's consent; explain to him or her the nature and purpose of your interview and respect your subject's confidentiality by allowing your subject to remain anonymous if he or she asks to be unnamed.

During your interview try to obtain as much information as you can about the following:

1. The subject's situation at the time of the deviance: age, employment, family situation, personal problems, and so on.
2. The subject's background: education, religion, family, and social class.
3. The actual situation in which the deviant act occurred: alone or with others, spur of the moment or planned.
4. The purpose of the deviation: fun, material gain, the venting of anger, and so on.
5. Has the deviation been repeated? If so, why? If not, why not?
6. Was the subject caught? If so, what happened?

After your interview has been conducted, attempt to explain this deviation by using some of the theories you have studied. Focus upon the mechanisms of social control that may or may not have been effective. Does this case seem to fit a particular theory, or does your explanation entail components of several theories? Do any theories fail to fit this case at all? Attempt to develop your own theory of deviance applicable to this situation.

CHAPTER 9
Concepts and Theories of Stratification

Overview

This largely theoretical chapter describes modern social theories
of stratification. It opens with a discussion of Marx's two-
class model and then discusses Weber's three-dimensional approach
to social class. It describes Lenski's theory of status
inconsistency and cites related research findings. It
distinguishes between ascribed and achieved statuses and
differentiates between structural and exchange mobility. Chapter
9 then turns its attention to Marx's utopian classless society
and Dahrendorf's critique of Marx. After Mosca's theory of the
inevitability of stratification is summarized, the chapter
examines the functionalist, social evolutionary, and conflict
approaches to stratification. Throughout the discussion of these
theoretical approaches, an example of a toy society illustrates
various concepts and assumptions. This chapter offers a more in-
depth explanation of many of the concepts introduced in Chapter
2. It also sets the stage for many of the chapters that follow.

Capsule Summary

Social stratification, the unequal distribution of rewards in a
society, has long been the subject of considerable interest.
Divisions of wealth and rank within societies are termed social
classes.
    Karl Marx, who developed the first modern social theory of
stratification, viewed class from the economic dimension. To
Marx, class membership was based on one's relationship to the
means of production. Those who own the means of production were
termed bourgeoisie and those who work it were termed proletariat.
Class membership was defined by both one's material position in
society and one's class consciousness. Marx was a utopian who
argued for a classless society based on the abolition of private
property. In his critique of Marx, Dahrendorf argued that
communistic societies are only classless by definition.
Stratification in these societies is based on control rather than
ownership of the means of production.
    Weber argued for a broader definition of class. To Weber,
class membership was determined by three dimensions: class (also
termed property), status (also called prestige), and power.
People disproportionately high (or low) on one dimension are
termed status inconsistent. Research has found that status
inconsistent people may experience psychological stress and often
favor politically liberal causes.
    Status may be based on achievement or ascription. Caste
systems rely mainly on ascription whereas industrialized
societies rely more heavily on achievement. Social mobility,

which results from changes in the distribution of statuses, is termed structural mobility. Mobility that is not structural is called exchange mobility.

Mosca argued that stratification is the inevitable result of political organization, which fosters inequalities in power and allows those with greater power to exploit others for material advantage.

The functional, social evolutionary, and conflict theories differ in their assumptions, yet all assume that some degree of stratification is inevitable. Functionalists argue that the stratification system ensures that functionally important positions will be filled because those occupying such positions will be highly rewarded. The concepts of functional importance and the principle of replaceability are central to the functionalist explanation. Social evolutionists argue that cultural accumulation results in a division of labor and specialization. This, in turn, leads to stratification. Conflict theorists argue that societies are even more stratified than necessary because those in powerful positions use their power to exploit the less powerful. Labor unions and professions, for example, use their power to control replaceability and ensure their own continuation of power.

Key Concepts

You should be able to explain the concepts listed here. You should also be able to cite several examples of each concept.

Key Research Studies

You should be familiar with both the methodology and the results of the tests of the theory of status inconsistency by the following researchers.

Key Theories

Be prepared to explain the assumptions of these theories and, when applicable, cite related research findings.

   Marx: stratification
   Weber: stratification
   Lenski: status inconsistency theory
   Dahrendorf: critique of Marx
   Mosca: stratification
   Davis and Moore: functionalist viewpoint
   Evolutionary perspective
   Conflict perspective

_____
Completion

1. Upward or downward movement by individuals or groups within a stratification system is termed _____.

2. Divisions of rank and wealth within societies are termed _____.

3. Marx called the class of people who work the means of production the _____.

4. Marx termed the very bottom of society's stratification system the _____.

5. Marx termed the tendency for workers to believe they had common interests with the ruling class _____.

6. Marx's definition of class is determined only by the _____ dimension.

7. Weber termed the three dimensions of stratification _____, _____, and _____.

8. According to Weber, _____ are groups of people with similar chances as determined by their economic position in society.

9. The ability to get one's way despite the resistance of others is _____.

10. Modern social scientists consider the "Three Ps" of stratification to be _____, _____, and _____.

11. Certain individual or group traits that determine status are termed _____.

12. Persons or groups who hold different ranks on each of the three dimensions are called _____.

13. Jackson hypothesized that _____ can have mental health consequences.

14. _____ status is based on merit while _____ status is a position based on who you are.

15. Social mobility that results from changes in the distribution of statuses in society is called _____.

16. A(n) _____ constructs plans for an ideal society.

17. _____ argued that stratification cannot be avoided since it is an inescapable feature of collective life.

18. A position is of high functional importance to a society to the degree that either the _____ or its _____ are hard to replace.

19. _____ theories focus on how stratification systems are subject to distortion.

20. _____ argue that the accumulation of culture inevitably leads to a division of labor and therefore to stratification.

_____
Multiple Choice

1. Marx termed those who own the means of production:
   a. the bourgeoisie
   b. the proletariat
   c. the Lumpenproletariat
   d. the middle class
   e. none of the above

2. Which of the following groups was not incorporated into Marx's class system?
   a. the owners of the means of production
   b. farmers and peasants
   c. the Lumpenproletariat
   d. b and c
   e. all of the above

3. Marx defined the two classes on the basis of:
   a. their material position in society
   b. prestige
   c. power
   d. a and c
   e. all of the above

4. What Weber called <u>class</u> modern social scientists refer to as:
   a. prestige
   b. status
   c. property
   d. power
   e. none of the above

5. The ability to get one's way despite the resistance of others is termed:
   a. property
   b. class
   c. status
   d. prestige
   e. none of the above

6. When famous sports stars endorse a commercial product, they are exchanging their _____ for economic advantage.
   a. property
   b. prestige
   c. power
   d. class
   e. position

7. Which of the following would be <u>most</u> likely to experience status inconsistency?
   a. a white male lawyer
   b. a black engineer with a doctorate
   c. a female physician
   d. a and c
   e. b and c

8. Research in the area of status inconsistency has found that:
   a. upper status blacks are more radical than lower status blacks
   b. Jewish bankers and industrialists have a record of voting for conservative parties
   c. wealthy and powerful American Catholics have a strong preference for the Republican party
   d. all of the above
   e. none of the above

9. Jackson measured status inconsistency on the basis of:
   a. occupation
   b. education
   c. racial-ethnic background
   d. a and b
   e. all of the above

10. Jackson's data found that:
    a. status inconsistency can have mental health consequences
    b. different patterns of inconsistency had different outcomes
    c. people of high status backgrounds with low status jobs had a high affinity for liberal politics and blamed the system for their failures
    d. a and b
    e. all of the above

11. When a society uses ascriptive status rules, people may be placed in status positions based on:
    a. place of birth
    b. family background
    c. sex
    d. b and c
    e. all of the above

12. In a caste system:
    a. status is based entirely on ascription
    b. ascription is the overwhelming basis for status
    c. status is based entirely on achievement
    d. achievement is the overwhelming basis for status
    e. none of the above

13. Exchange mobility:
    a. is common when the acriptive status rule operates
    b. is very uncommon when status is based on achievement
    c. is very common regardless of the rules governing status
    d. a and b
    e. none of the above

14. Marx argued that in order to achieve a classless society:
    a. the proletariat should own the means of production
    b. the state should be abolished
    c. private ownership of the means of production should be abolished
    d. the bourgeoisie should own the means of production
    e. none of the above

15. Mosca argued that:
    a. human societies cannot exist without political organization
    b. whenever there is political organization, there must be inequalities in power
    c. a classless society is possible if private ownership is abolished
    d. a and b
    e. b and c

16. The functionalist view of stratification argues that:
    a. positions in society differ in the degree to which they are functionally important
    b. some positions are inherently more difficult to fill adequately to ensure an adequate supply of people in important positions
    c. to ensure an adequate supply of people to fill important positions, it is necessary to attach higher rewards to those positions
    d. all of the above
    e. none of the above

17. Which of the following theorists is/are correctly paired with his view or theory of stratification?
    a. Marx: conflict theory
    b. Davis and Moore: social evolutionary
    c. Lenski: functionalist theory
    d. all of the above
    e. none of the above

18. A position is of high functional importance when:
    a. the position itself is hard to replace
    b. the occupants of the position are hard to replace
    c. its functions can be performed by people in other positions
    d. a and b
    e. all of the above

19. _____ theory takes the premise that the accumulation of culture results in cultural specialization, which in turn results in stratification.
    a. Functionalist
    b. Social evolutionary
    c. Conflict
    d. Marxist
    e. Weberian

20. Most modern conflict theorists:
    a. argue that stratification is unavoidable
    b. asume that people who are in a position to exploit others will do so
    c. argue that societies are more stratified than necessary
    d. b and c
    e. all of the above

Essay

1. A. List the three theories of stratification. (knowledge)
   B. Explain the three theories of stratification. (comprehension)
   C. Compare and contrast two of these theories. (analysis)

2. A. Define the principle of replaceability. (knowledge)
   B. Give examples of the politics of replaceability from labor unions and the professions. (comprehension)
   C. Apply this principle to the toy society. (application)

3. Contrast Marx and Weber on the subject of social class.

4. Discuss the concept of status inconsistency. Cite some research finding on this topic.

5. Discuss Marx on the classless society and explain Dahrendorf's critique of Marx.

Answers

Completion

1. social mobility
2. social classes
3. proletariat
4. <u>Lumpenproletariat</u>
5. false consciousness
6. economic
7. class, status, power
8. classes
9. power
10. property, prestige, power
11. status characteristics
12. status inconsistent
13. status inconsistency
14. Achieved, ascribed
15. structural mobility
16. utopian
17. Mosca
18. position itself, occupants
19. Conflict
20. Evolutionary theories

Multiple Choice

1. b
2. d
3. a
4. c
5. e
6. b
7. e
8. a
9. e
10. d
11. e
12. b
13. e
14. c
15. d
16. d
17. e
18. d
19. b
20. e

CHAPTER 10
Comparing Systems of Stratification

Overview

This chapter contrasts the stratification systems of hunting and gathering, agrarian, and industrialized societies. It starts with a description of hunting and gathering societies and then describes the changes brought about by the advent of agrarian societies. It also describes the stratification systems of agrarian societies and examines the differences between the elite and the masses. Chapter 10 then discusses the changes in the stratification system brought about by industrialization, focusing on research findings about mobility in industrialized nations. The chapter is followed by a special topic on the rise of military domination in feudal Europe. Many of the concepts first introduced in Chapters 2 and 9 are applied to the various stratification systems.

Capsule Summary

Stratification exists in all societies, even the simplest hunting and gathering societies composed of small bands of people who wander in search of food. They are the least stratified of all societies and have few possessions, no full-time leaders, and little role specialization. Stratification is typically based on age and sex, although within the sexes it is often based on achieved characteristics.
     As societies became more complex they became more stratified. Agrarian societies fostered the rise of specialization, personal property, government, cities, and slavery. These societies were highly stratified with large gaps separating the elite from the masses. Agrarian societies were dominated by the military and were in a chronic state of warfare.
     Industrialization changed the stratification system. Societies became less stratified. The gap between the top and bottom decreased as the middle classes expanded and jobs for unskilled labor began to disappear. As more skill and training were required for jobs, positions and their occupants became less replaceable; workers thus became more powerful and better able to resist coercion. The rise of democracy and industrialization went hand in hand.
     Research has found high rates of structural mobility in industrialized nations. Compared with European nations, the United States has higher rates of long-distance mobility. Recent research by Blau and Duncan and by Porter has focused upon status attainment in the United States and Canada and the application of the status attainment model to mobility in these nations. The results of this research have yielded some surprising results. Although earlier studies of mobility focused only upon the male,

more recent studies have also focused upon <u>female mobility</u> and <u>status attainment</u>.

Key Concepts

You should be able to explain the following concepts; be ready to provide several examples of each concept.

Hunting and gathering
   society   254
Agrarian society   257
Specialization   257
Industrialization   263
Industrial society   263

Structural mobility   266
Long-distance mobility   266
Status attainment model   268
Feudalism (included in
   Special Topic 3)   275

Key Research Studies

Be familiar with both the methodology and the results of the research studies cited here.

Lipset and Bendix: comparative social mobility   266
Blau and Duncan: comparison of rates of long-distance
                mobility   266
Blau and Duncan: status attainment model   267
Porter and others: status attainment in Canada   268

Key Theories

You should be able to explain the assumptions of these theories as they apply to stratification in industrial societies; when applicable, cite related research findings.

Functionalism
Conflict theory

In addition to these theories, you should be <u>thoroughly</u> familiar with stratification systems of:

Hunting and gathering societies
Agrarian societies
Industrial societies

Completion

1. The simplest type of society is the _____ society.

2. Recent archeological discoveries in Africa indicate that humans existed more than _____ ago.

3. The primary bases for stratification in hunting and gathering societies are age and _____.

4. Within age and sex groups, simple societies are not very _____.

5. With the invention of plows and effective animal harnesses, _____ societies appeared.

6. The advent of agriculture made possible _____ and _____.

7. _____ societies lived in a chronic state of warfare.

8. Because agrarian societies were based on _____, they tended to be expansionistic.

9. The most stratified societies are typically _____ societies.

10. Industrial societies are not based on getting people to work harder but to _____.

11. Using technology to make work much more productive is termed _____.

12. As positions become _____ replaceable, their relative rewards increase.

13. As a consequence of industrialization, the average worker is more _____ and thus more able to resist coercion.

14. Compared to agrarian societies, industrial societies are _____ stratified.

15. Bendix and Lipset observed that in industrial societies there is a great deal of _____ mobility.

16. _____ mobility involves huge upward or downward shifts in status.

17. Blau and Duncan found a very strong correlation between _____ and occupational status.

18. Studies of status attainment in Canada have found that it is very _____ to that of the United States.

19. Studies have found that female _____ is not very different from that of men.

Note: The next question is drawn from Special Topic 3.

20.   In feudal societies, land ownership is based on _____.

Multiple Choice

1.   The simplest form of society is the _____ society.
     a.   gardening
     b.   hunting and gathering
     c.   agrarian
     d.   industrial
     e.   herding

2.   The least stratified societies are:
     a.   agrarian societies
     b.   hunting and gathering societies
     c.   industrialized societies
     d.   herding societies
     e.   horticultural societies

3.   In a hunting and gathering society:
     a.   there is extensive role specialization
     b.   power is based on land ownership
     c.   stratification is generally based on sex and age
     d.   a and c
     e.   all of the above

4.   The rule seems to be that the _____ a human society is, the less it is stratified.
     a.   smaller
     b.   poorer
     c.   more secure
     d.   a and b
     e.   all of the above

5.   Improved agriculture produced:
     a.   warfare
     b.   cities
     c.   surplus food production
     d.   b and c
     e.   all of the above

6.   Slavery is most likely to be found in:
     a.   hunting and gathering societies
     b.   agrarian societies
     c.   industrialized societies
     d.   a and b
     e.   all of the above

7.   The ability to produce surplus food may lead to:
     a.   humans becoming property
     b.   a more extensive division of labor
     c.   government
     d.   all of the above
     e.   none of the above

8. In an agrarian society, the masses and the elite may differ in:
    a. language
    b. ethnic background
    c. the amount of time devoted to leisure activities
    d. a and c
    e. all of the above

9. The most highly stratified societies tend to be:
    a. agrarian
    b. herding
    c. gardening
    d. industrialized
    e. b and c

10. Changes in the stratification system brought about by industrialization include:
    a. a widening of the gap between the masses and the elite
    b. greater replaceability of positions
    c. a decrease in the power of the average worker, who is less able to resist coercion
    d. all of the above
    e. none of the above

11. Which of the following statements is/are true?
    a. As positions become less replaceable, their relative rewards decrease.
    b. To the extent that occupational positions require education and training, they are less replaceable.
    c. In the long run, industrialization has made the average worker more replaceable.
    d. a and c
    e. all of the above

12. As a consequence of industrialization:
    a. people "work smarter"
    b. the average worker has become less replaceable
    c. the training necessary to do most jobs has enabled workers to demand a higher level of reward
    d. all of the above
    e. none of the above

13. Differences between industrialized and agrarian societies include the fact that:
    a. industrial societies are more stratified
    b. industrial societies are less stratified
    c. the gap between the poor and the wealthy is greater in an industrial society
    d. a and c
    e. b and c

14. Bendix and Lipset found that:
    a. there is much more structural mobility in the United States than in other industrialized democracies
    b. there is more exchange mobility in the United States than in other industrialized democracies
    c. the amount of exchange mobility in the United States is about equal to that of other industrialized democracies
    d. a and c
    e. none of the above

15. Huge upward or downward shifts in status are termed _____ mobility.
    a. exchange
    b. structural
    c. long-distance
    d. vertical
    e. horizontal

16. Blau and Duncan (status attainment model) found that:
    a. it's better to start at the top than at the bottom of the stratification system
    b. the primary mechanism linking the occupational status of fathers and sons is education
    c. family background is a more important influence on status attainment than is education
    d. a and b
    e. a and c

17. Studies of status attainment in Canada have found that:
    a. Canada's rate of social mobility is almost identical to that of the United States
    b. opportunities for occupational advancement in Canada are much more restricted than in most industrialized nations
    c. ethnicity plays a major role in status attainment
    d. all of the above
    e. b and c

18. Studies of female status attainment in Canada have shown that:
    a. native-born Canadian women with full-time jobs come from lower status family backgrounds than do their male counterparts
    b. the average native-born Canadian woman has a higher status occupation than do similar men
    c. the correlations between women's occupational prestige and their fathers' occupational prestige are much lower than for men
    d. b and c
    e. all of the above

Note: The following two questions are drawn from Special Topic 3.

94

19. In feudal societies, land ownership is based on _____ obligations.
    a. economic
    b. kinship
    c. military
    d. religious
    e. none of the above

20. The inequalities of agrarian societies arose when _____ specialists emerged.
    a. agricultural
    b. military
    c. religious
    d. artistic
    e. none of the above

Essay

1. A. List the three types of societies. (knowledge)
   B. Explain the stratification systems in each of these societies. (comprehension)
   C. Contrast the stratification systems of hunting and gathering societies with those of agrarian societies. (analysis)

2. A. Explain the stratification systems in agrarian and industrialized societies. (comprehension)
   B. Show how industrialization changed the stratification system. (application)
   C. Contrast the stratification systems of these two societies. (analysis)

3. Discuss some of the research findings on social mobility.

4. Explain the following statement: "The smaller, the poorer, and the less secure society is, the less it is stratified."

5. Show how the adoption of the stirrup led to the rise of feudalism and military domination. (This question is drawn from Special Topic 3.)

_____
Answers

Completion

1.	hunting and gathering	11.	industrialization
2.	3 million years	12.	less
3.	sex	13.	powerful
4.	stratified	14.	less
5.	agrarian	15.	structural
6.	specialization, cities	16.	Long-distance
7.	Agrarian	17.	education
8.	military rule	18.	similar
9.	agrarian	19.	status attainment
10.	work smarter	20.	military obligations

Multiple Choice

1.	b	11.	b
2.	b	12.	d
3.	c	13.	b
4.	d	14.	b
5.	e	15.	c
6.	b	16.	d
7.	d	17.	a
8.	e	18.	d
9.	a	19.	c
10.	e	20.	b

CHAPTER 11
Intergroup Conflict: Racial and Ethnic Inequality

Overview

Chapter 11 opens with a discussion of intergroup conflict and mechanisms for reducing these conflicts. It explains early theories such as authoritarianism, which argued that conflict results from prejudice. Then it focuses on more recent explanations such as Allport's contact theory, which argued that prejudice results from social inequality and competition. Using examples, the chapter shows how inequality and economic competition may lead to prejudice. This chapter also looks at slavery and its aftermath and discusses Myrdal's An American Dilemma. The decline of prejudice is then discussed with such examples as the Japanese immigrants in the United States and Canada. The chapter also considers today's minorities and analyzes their plight and recent progress from the perspective of "new immigrants." Following the chapter is a special topic that focuses on minority participation in sports and entertaiment as a mechanism for overcoming discrimination.

Capsule Summary

Prejudice is often the result of intergroup conflict and status inequality. Intergroup conflict may include both racial and ethnic groups. This conflict may be resolved through assimilation, accommodation (and hence pluralism), extermination or expulsion of the weaker group, or the imposition of a caste system. Earlier theories such as the authoritarian personality theory argued that prejudice caused intergroup conflict. More recent theories argued that the reverse is correct.

Allport's contact theory argued that contact between groups will reduce prejudice if the two groups meet on the basis of equal status and pursue common goals. Research has supported this claim. Conditions imposed by slavery and its aftermath (sometimes termed "an American dilemma") illustrate the reverse of this theory. Inequality, economic competition, and the imposition of a caste system can increase prejudice. Minorities do not always occupy the lowest status. Middleman minorities frequently are a buffer between the highest and lowest classes and are often the targets of their frustration.

Historically, many minorities have achieved upward mobility through the mechanisms of geographic concentration, internal economic development, occupational specialization, and the development of a middle class. Japanese-Americans and Japanese-Canadians are prime examples. Some minorities have used sports or the entertainment fields to overcome the barriers of prejudice and discrimination.

Today's minorities--blacks, Native Americans, and Chicanos, for example--differ from other minorities in that they have resided in the United States and Canada for many generations. Still they have been treated almost as a caste apart from mainstream society. For this reason many sociologists view them as recent immigrants and analyze their recent progress from that standpoint. Blacks, for example, were once concentrated in the rural South, where they received little education or training necessary for upward mobility in an urban, industrialized society. They have been further hampered by their visibility, large population, lack of a homeland, and the legacies of slavery. Prejudice still exists although recent gains by these minorities are similar to those made in the past by newly arrived immigrant groups.

Key Concepts

You should be able to explain the concepts listed here, as well as cite several examples of each concept.

Intergroup conflict 279	Segregation 281
Race 279	Prejudice 282
Ethnic group 279	Authoritarian
Assimilation 280	personality 282
Accommodation 281	Cultural division of
Expulsion 281	labor 295
Extermination 281	Middleman minorities 295
Cultural (ethnic) pluralism 281	Visibility 311

Key Research Studies

Be familiar with both the methodology and the results of the following research studies.

Sherif and Sherif: artificial inducement of prejudice   284
Various studies of the relationship between prejudice and other variables (throughout chapter)

Key Figures

You should be able to associate each person with his contribution.

Charles Darwin: biological theory of evolution
Gunnar Myrdal: An American Dilemma
Gordon Allport: The Nature of Prejudice

Key Theories

Be prepared to explain the assumptions of these theories and, when
applicable, cite related research findings. Blalock's theory
appears in Special Topic 4.

> Allport's theory of contact
> Theories of prejudice: authoritarian personality; contact;
>   status inequality
> Bonacich's model: labor and minorities
> Three mechanisms that foster upward mobility
> Blacks as recent immigrants
> Blalock's explanation of minorities' success in sports

In addition, you should be <u>thoroughly</u> familiar with the
experiences of the various minorities discussed in this chapter.

Completion

1. A human group with some observable common biological features
    that set it off from other human groups is termed a(n)
    _____.

2. Ethnic groups are groups whose _____ differ.

3. For a long time it was believed that intergroup conflicts in
    North America would be resolved through _____.

4. When intergroup conflict ends through _____, the result
    is ethnic or cultural pluralism.

5. Besides accommodation and assimilation, the possible outcomes
    of intergroup conflict include _____, _____, and
    _____.

6. Until very recently, most social scientists regarded
    _____ as the cause of intergroup conflict.

7. Adorno argued that prejudice was the result of a(n)
    _____ personality type.

8. Contact theory is most closely associated with _____.

9. Allport argued that prejudice will _____ if two groups
    are engaged in competition.

10. The more highly _____ a person is and the higher a
    person's _____, the less likely a person is to be
    prejudiced against other racial and ethnic groups.

11. Myrdal's <u>An American Dilemma</u> dealt with the contradiction
    between _____ and _____.

12. There is no greater status inequality than that between
    _____ and _____.

13. Lieberson concluded that fear of blacks as _____ is the
    real cause of racial stereotypes.

14. According to Bonacich, factors that lead subordinate groups
    to work for substandard wages include a low standard of
    living, a lack of political power, _____, and
    _____.

15. A minority group that serves as both a link and a buffer
    between the upper and lower classes is referred to as a
    _____ minority.

16. Sociologists today consider the experience of blacks in
    America to be similar to that of _____.

17. When racial or ethnic groups tend to specialize in a few
    occupations, it is termed a(n) _____.

18. The degree to which a racial or ethnic group can be
    recognized is termed _____.

19. Barriers to black progress include the legacies of slavery,
    _____, visibility, and _____.

Note: The next question is drawn from Special Topic 4.

20. Blalock argued that when employers compete intensely for
    talented people they will be _____ likely to
    discriminate.

_____

Multiple Choice

1. Races may differ on the basis of:
   a. skin color
   b. eyelid shape
   c. blood type
   d. a and b
   e. all of the above

2. Possible outcomes of intergroup conflict include:
   a. accommodation
   b. expulsion of the weaker group
   c. the imposition of a caste system
   d. a and b
   e. all of the above

3. Ethnic groups are:
   a. groups whose cultural heritage differ from other groups within the same society
   b. involuntary groups since people don't choose to join them
   c. groups that share observable biological differences
   d. a and b
   e. a and c

4. When intergroup conflict ends through accommodation, the result is:
   a. ethnic or cultural pluralism
   b. assimilation
   c. expulsion of the weaker group
   d. all of the above
   e. none of the above

5. The theory that some people are so oversocialized that they accept only their group's norms and values argues that prejudice is the result of:
   a. intergroup conflict
   b. status inequality
   c. competitive contact with others
   d. the authoritarian personality
   e. none of the above

6. Contact theory is most closely associated with:
   a. Gordon Allport
   b. Gunnar Myrdal
   c. Thomas Sowell
   d. H. M. Blalock
   e. none of the above

7. According to contact theory, prejudice will _intensify_ when groups:
   a. possess equal status
   b. cooperate to pursue common goals
   c. are engaged in competition
   d. a and b
   e. all of the above

8. _An American Dilemma_ was written by:
   a. Gordon Allport
   b. Gunnar Myrdal
   c. Muzafer Sherif
   d. Thomas Sowell
   e. H. M. Blalock

9. Today most sociologists view status inequality as:
   a. the cause of prejudice but the result of discrimination
   b. the cause of, not the result of, prejudice and discrimination
   c. the result of prejudice and discrimination
   d. the cause of discrimination and the result of prejudice
   e. none of the above

10. Lieberson believes that the real <u>cause</u> of racial stereotypes is:
    a. fear of black and white intermarriage
    b. differences in skin color
    c. prejudice and discrimination
    d. fear of blacks as economic competitors
    e. none of the above

11. Bonacich argued that factors that often cause or require members of subordinate groups to work for substandard wages include:
    a. a low standard of living
    b. a lack of information
    c. a lack of political power
    d. all of the above
    e. a and c

12. Strategies used to prevent a subordinate group from competing economically with the dominant group include:
    a. exclusion
    b. the establishment of a caste system
    c. accommodation
    d. a and b
    e. all of the above

13. Middleman minorities:
    a. may serve as a link between the upper and lower classes
    b. may serve as a buffer between the upper and lower classes
    c. may defuse potential class conflicts by becoming the focus of frustration and anger
    d. b and c
    e. all of the above

14. The typical occupation for first-generation Japanese-Canadians and Japanese-Americans was:
    a. farming and gardening
    b. mining
    c. garment work
    d. jewelry making
    e. none of the above

15. Mechanisms by which minorities have achieved upward mobility include:
    a. occupational generalization
    b. geographical concentration
    c. the development of a middle class
    d. b and c
    e. all of the above

16. Internal economic development by minorities is often enhanced by:
    a. the founding of their own financial institutions
    b. geographic diffusion
    c. buying outside of their own community
    d. all of the above
    e. none of the above

17. Until recently, blacks in the United States:
    a. lived mainly in the South
    b. lived mainly in urban areas
    c. had a low level of education
    d. a and c
    e. all of the above

18. Barriers to black progress and upward mobility include:
    a. the legacies of slavery
    b. the lack of a homeland
    c. their visibility
    d. all of the above
    e. none of the above

19. The degree to which a racial or ethnic group can be recognized is termed:
    a. identifiability
    b. visibility
    c. outward indication
    d. openness
    e. none of the above

20. When racial equality has been achieved:
    a. all members of each group must be of the same status
    b. the distribution of their members in the social structure is the same
    c. a person's race does not reliably indicate his or her status
    d. a and b
    e. b and c

Essay

1. A. Name three ways in which intergroup conflict may be resolved. (knowledge)
   B. Explain Allport's contact theory. (comprehension)
   C. Apply Allport's theory to a fictitious situation in a school or work setting. (application)

2. A. Name three ways in which minorities may achieve upward mobility. (knowledge)
   B. Explain Blalock's model. (comprehension)
   C. Apply this model to show how minorities often overcome discrimination in sports and entertainment. (application)

3. Using an example, show how economic inequalities and status differences can lead to prejudice.

4. Trace the experiences of Japanese-Canadians or Japanese-Americans from their initial arrival in North America to their position in Canadian or American society today. Be certain to integrate into your explanation the various mechanisms by which minorities may achieve upward mobility.

5. Trace the experiences of blacks in America from slavery to the present. Show how their position may be likened to that of recent immigrants.

Answers

Completion

1.	race	11.	democratic ideals, racist practices
2.	cultural heritages	12.	master, slave
3.	assimilation	13.	economic competitors
4.	accommodation	14.	a lack of information, economic motives
5.	extermination, expulsion, the imposition of a caste system	15.	middleman
6.	prejudice	16.	recent immigrants
7.	authoritarian	17.	cultural division of labor
8.	Gordon Allport	18.	visibility
9.	intensify	19.	no homeland, numbers
10.	educated, income	20.	less

Multiple Choice

1.	e	11.	d
2.	e	12.	d
3.	d	13.	e
4.	a	14.	a
5.	d	15.	d
6.	a	16.	a
7.	c	17.	d
8.	b	18.	d
9.	b	19.	b
10.	d	20.	e

CHAPTERS 9 TO 11
Review and Special Project

Review

This section has focused on social inequality and social stratification. It has discussed various sociological theories of stratification, different stratification systems, and the consequences of social inequality.

Special Project

The various social classes (and even groups occupying the different strata within the classes) often exhibit marked differences in life-style. Although these differences are not nearly as great as those that separated the classes in agrarian societies, they nevertheless continue to exist. Research has shown that the classes differ not only in obvious ways such as income and educational level but also in more subtle areas such as speech patterns, mortality rates, types of entertainment, and even preferences for particular brands of beer.

You may wish to speculate about some aspects of life-style that might exhibit class differences. Choose one or two areas and devise specific hypotheses about the nature of these relationships. Search the literature for studies that test your hypotheses. (Bibliographies in sociology texts would be a good place to begin your literature search. You will also want to consult the Sociological Abstracts during your study.)

If possible, you may also wish to obtain your own data through observation, interviews, or more unobtrusive measures such as noting television commercials and magazine advertisements geared to a target population. Once you have supported your hypothesis, you might explain this relationship by using some of the theories you have studied.

CHAPTER 12
The Family

Overview

This chapter opens with a discussion of the dominant themes of the universality and the decline of the family. It then offers definitions of <u>family</u> and differentiates between nuclear and extended families. It discusses the four functions of the family before turning to a discussion of the traditional preindustrial European family. The theme of modernization (a major emphasis in later chapters) is discussed with emphasis on the transformation of the family and the effects of modernization on kinship and divorce. Chapter 12 also considers one-parent families. Patterson's work on the relationship between parenting practices and childhood deviance is highlighted as the "over-the-shoulder" example. (Again, the importance of attachments is emphasized in this research.) The chapter closes with a discussion of research on remarriage. A special topic on college couples follows this chapter.

Capsule Summary

<u>Families</u> are small clusters of males and females, adults and children. <u>Membership</u> is typically <u>determined</u> by <u>common ancestry</u> and <u>sexual unions</u>. Although its form may differ, the family appears to be <u>universal</u>. <u>Family forms</u> include both the <u>nuclear</u> and the <u>extended</u> family. <u>Families</u> typically perform the <u>functions</u> of <u>reproduction</u>, <u>sexual regulation</u>, <u>economic cooperation</u>, and <u>education</u>. The <u>incest taboo</u> exists in every culture although its form also differs among cultures.

It has been assumed that the family is experiencing <u>decline</u> although recent research by <u>Shorter</u> found the <u>traditional European family</u> to be almost the <u>exact opposite</u> of the <u>large, close, loving, extended family</u> it was long thought to be. Families were <u>smaller</u> than originally thought because <u>infant</u> and <u>childhood mortality were high</u>, <u>children left home early</u>, and <u>adults often died before becoming old</u>. <u>Privacy</u> was <u>nonexistent</u>; families lived in one room often shared with outsiders. <u>Attachments between parents</u> and <u>children</u> were <u>weak</u> and neglect was common. Relationships between <u>spouses</u> were <u>indifferent</u> or <u>hostile</u>. Peer group bonds were strong and served as the primary emotional attachments. <u>Modernization</u> brought about major <u>changes</u>. <u>Romantic love</u> rather than economic ties became the basis for <u>marriage</u>; emotional bonds between <u>children</u> and <u>parents</u> also were strengthened. The family of today is a result of these changes.

The <u>divorce rate</u> has risen markedly. Factors contributing to this rise include the <u>emphasis</u> upon <u>romantic love</u> as the primary bond between spouses, the <u>entrance</u> of large numbers of <u>women</u> into the <u>work force</u>, and the <u>increased opportunity to obtain a divorce</u>.

Since approximately <u>two-thirds of all divorces occur among couples</u> who have <u>children</u>, much attention has been focused on the <u>one-parent family</u>. <u>One-parent families</u> result not only from <u>divorce</u> but also from the <u>death of a spouse</u> and from the <u>increasing number of single women becoming mothers</u>. Most one-parent homes are headed by <u>women</u>, and problems with <u>money</u> and <u>time</u> often plague the single parent.

It has often been assumed that children from one-parent homes are more prone to delinquency, but research in this area has produced mixed results. <u>Patterson</u>, in his study of <u>deviant children</u>, found that the deviance is a result of <u>poor parenting</u> rather than family structure. <u>Parents</u> of <u>deviant children</u> often <u>lack close attachments</u> to them and often <u>deny</u> or <u>fail</u> to <u>punish their children's deviant acts</u>.

More than <u>80 percent</u> of Canadians and Americans who divorce remarry. Recently research has been conducted on <u>conjugal careers</u>, and studies such as those by <u>Jacobs and Furstenberg</u> and <u>White and Booth</u> have focused upon the <u>economic characteristics</u> of second spouses and the <u>impact of stepchildren in the home</u>.

Key Concepts

Be prepared to explain the concepts listed here. You should be able to provide several examples of each concept.

Key Research Studies

You should be familiar with both the methodology and the results of the following research studies. The study by Hill and others appears in Special Topic 5.

1. Sociological writing on the family has been dominated by the themes of _____ and _____.

2. The four primary functions of the family include sexual relationships, reproduction, _____, and _____.

3. A formal commitment to maintain a long-term relationship involving specific rights and responsibilities is termed _____.

4. An adult couple and their children is a(n) _____ family.

5. Virtually every society contains a(n) _____, which prohibits sexual relations between certain family members.

6. Family members such as the elderly and children who cannot support themselves are termed _____.

7. _____ wrote The Making of the Modern Family.

8. The primary unit of sociability and attachment in the traditional European family was the _____.

9. The high divorce rate indicates that the marital relationship has become much _____ important than it used to be.

10. Approximately _____ of divorces occur among couples who have children.

11. Sociologists attribute the high divorce rates to the fact that romance is a highly perishable commodity and _____.

12. Women who are age 30 and older when they give birth to their first child are termed _____.

13. The proportion of children born to unwed mothers is termed the _____.

14. More than 90 percent of one-parent families are headed by _____.

15. Research has found that _____ is a primary cause of deviant behavior among children.

16. A major problem faced by female-headed families is lack of _____.

17. A major problem experienced by parents with poor parenting skills is a lack of _____ to their children.

18. More than _____ percent of Canadians and Americans who divorce remarry.

19. On the average, women marry second husbands who are _____ successful than their first husbands.

20. If there are no stepchildren in the home, couples who remarry _____ have a higher rate of divorce than people who are marrying for the first time.

Multiple Choice

1. Murdock defined the family as a social group characterized by:
   a. common residence
   b. adults of both sexes
   c. reproduction
   d. a and c
   e. all of the above

2. Primary functions of the family include:
   a. economic cooperation among members
   b. sexual relationships
   c. reproduction
   d. b and c
   e. all of the above

3. An extended family is:
   a. larger than a nuclear family
   b. composed of more than one nuclear family
   c. composed of an adult couple and its children
   d. a and b
   e. none of the above

4. The theme of the decline of the family:
   a. has been supported by recent research by Shorter
   b. argues that the functions of the family are best met by the modern family
   c. is obvious when the contemporary family is compared with the traditional family
   d. a and c
   e. none of the above

5. Which of the following is/are true about sexual gratification as a function of the family?
   a. All societies have norms governing sexual behavior.
   b. All societies have very narrow limits on who may engage in sex.
   c. Sexual norms often change very rapidly.
   d. a and c
   e. all of the above

6. Which of the following is/are research findings of Shorter's study?
    a. The extended family living in a single household was typical regardless of economic level.
    b. The traditional household was much smaller than had been assumed.
    c. Female-headed households were very rare compared to today.
    d. all of the above
    e. none of the above

7. Shorter found that the size of the traditional family was smaller than previously assumed because:
    a. infant and childhood mortality was high
    b. children often left home early
    c. adults often died before reaching "old age"
    d. a and c
    e. all of the above

8. Shorter found that relations between husbands and wives and parents and children:
    a. were based on emotional rather than economic ties
    b. were often characterized by indifference or even hostility
    c. were stronger than relationshps to peer group members
    d. a and c
    e. none of the above

9. In the traditional European family, strong emotional attachments were primarily between:
    a. persons of the same sex and outside the family
    b. mothers and young children
    c. husbands and wives
    d. elderly parents and adult children
    e. brothers and sisters

10. Effects of modernization on the family include:
    a. an increase in privacy for families
    b. a decrease in the importance of emotional ties as the basis for marriage
    c. an increase in the importance of peer group relations
    d. a and c
    e. none of the above

11. Shanas's research on the quality of kinship bonds in modern life found that:
    a. kinship ties have suffered greatly from the rise of urban industrial societies
    b. elderly adults typically maintain strong ties with their adult children
    c. elderly adults typically maintain weak ties with adult children
    d. a and c
    e. none of the above

12. More than _____ of those who divorce remarry.
    a. 10 percent
    b. 50 percent
    c. 80 percent
    d. 90 percent
    e. 98 percent

13. Approximately _____ of divorces occur between people who have had children.
    a. one-third
    b. two-thirds
    c. one-half
    d. three-quarters
    e. four-fifths

14. Factors that have led to an increased divorce rate include:
    a. the increased opportunity to get divorced
    b. an increase in the importance of emotional ties as the basis for marriage
    c. the increased financial independence of women
    d. a and c
    e. all of the above

15. "Mature mothers":
    a. are women who are age 30 and older when they give birth to their first child
    b. are typically poorly educated
    c. are overwhelmingly career women
    d. a and c
    e. all of the above

16. The recent influx of women into the labor force:
    a. contributes to a low birth rate
    b. has produced the phenomenon known as the "mature mother"
    c. reflects a low birth rate
    d. a and c
    e. all of the above

17. Patterson found that deviant children:
    a. had always been raised in a one-parent family
    b. were often greatly loved by their parents but that this attachment was not returned
    c. often had parents with poor parenting skills
    d. a and b
    e. none of the above

18. Patterson found that parents of problem children:
    a. have weak attachments to their children
    b. often fail to punish their children for failing to obey
    c. often refuse to "see" what their children are doing
    d. all of the above
    e. none of the above

19. According to Jacobs and Furstenberg:
    a. women overwhelmingly better their economic situation by remarriage
    b. women usually marry second husbands who are no more and no less successful than their first husbands
    c. a woman with children under 10 is in the best position to improve her economic situation by remarriage
    d. a and b
    e. a and c

20. According to research by White and Booth:
    a. stepchildren leave home at a younger age than do biological children
    b. couples who remarry have a higher divorce rate than people who are marrying for the first time if there are no stepchildren in the home
    c. couples who remarry do not have a higher rate of divorce than people who are marrying for the first time if there are no stepchildren in the home
    d. a and b
    e. a and c

Essay

1. A. Name the four functions of the family. (knowledge)
   B. Discuss the theme of the universality of the family. (comprehension)
   C. Contrast the nuclear family with the extended family. (analysis)

2. A. Discuss some of the characteristics of the traditional European family as described by Shorter. (comprehension)
   B. Contrast the typical view of the extended family with the traditional family described by Shorter. (application)
   C. Relate the theme of decline to your discussion. (analysis)

3. Explain the following statement: "The current high divorce rate . . . could mean that at any given moment the great majority of marriages are happy ones."

4. Describe the changes in the family brought about by modernization.

5. Describe Patterson's research on deviant children. Cite three of his tactics for improving parenting skills.

Answers

Completion

1. universality, decline
2. economic cooperation, education (socialization)
3. marriage
4. nuclear
5. incest taboo
6. dependents
7. Edward Shorter
8. peer group
9. more
10. two-thirds
11. the increased opportunities to get divorced
12. mature mothers
13. illegitimacy ratio
14. a female (or woman)
15. poor parenting
16. income
17. attachments
18. 80
19. no more, no less (equally as)
20. do not

Multiple Choice

1.	e	11.	b
2.	e	12.	c
3.	d	13.	b
4.	e	14.	e
5.	d	15.	d
6.	b	16.	e
7.	e	17.	c
8.	b	18.	d
9.	a	19.	b
10.	a	20.	e

CHAPTER 13
Religion

Overview

This chapter opens with a discussion of the nature of religion
and how it differs from other belief systems that offer answers
to questions about ultimate meaning. It describes how religion
makes norms legitimate and serves as a major force in creating
moral communities. It introduces the concept of a religious
economy and considers church-sect theory in depth. Chapter 13
discusses secularization and its effects on both sect revival and
cult formation. It also discusses the American religious economy
and cites numerous research findings by Stark and others about
sect and cult formation and concentration in both America and
Europe. A brief discussion of the universal appeal of religion
concludes the chapter. The importance of attachments is a
recurrent theme in this chapter and considerable attention is
paid to the relationship between attachments and religious
application.

Capsule Summary

Religion consists of socially organized patterns of beliefs and
practices concerning questions of ultimate meaning that assume
the existence of the supernatural. Evidence that religion existed
100,000 years ago has been found in the remains of Neanderthal
culture. Religion serves to make norms legitimate by explaining
why they exist and should be followed.
        As societies grew more complex, many different religions
emerged, often side by side, thus creating pluralistic religious
economies. Weber distinguished between the concepts of church
and sect. Further elaborations of church-sect theory by Niebuhr
and Johnson postulate that churches are characterized by
intellectualized teachings, emotional restraint in services, and
deities who are remote from human affairs. They exist in a state
of relatively low tension with the sociocultural environment.
Sects, on the other hand, embrace emotionalism, fundamentalism,
and personal relationships with deities. They tend to exist in a
state of high tension with the sociocultural environment.
        Secularization involves turning away from religion to a
secular view of life. Initially, many people thought that
increased secularization would lead to the eventual decline of
religion. Recent research has not supported this argument;
although secularization does lead to a decline in dominant
religious organizations such as churches, sects and cults often
emerge to take their place. Sects differ from cults in that
sects are revivals of an old religion. (The term revival is used
to indicate sect formation.) Cults, on the other hand, are new
religions and emerge as a result of innovation. Charisma is the

114

ability of some people to inspire faith in others, and <u>charismatic</u> <u>leaders</u> are often very instrumental in <u>religious movements</u>.

The <u>North American religious economy</u> is <u>very diverse</u>. <u>Church attendance</u> is <u>high</u>, and almost two-thirds of all North Americans are members of a local congregation. <u>Sect formation</u> is common since many of the dominant organizations are experiencing decline. <u>Sect movements</u> are clustered <u>where church membership is</u> <u>highest</u> because they represent a <u>revival</u> of an <u>already</u> <u>established religion</u>. Because <u>cults</u> represent a <u>new religion</u>, they experience greatest success in areas where <u>church attendance</u> <u>is low</u> such as in the "unchurched belt" of the Pacific coast. Cults often attract people who have no previous religious affiliation. Thus, rather than leading to a decline in religion itself, secularization has led to <u>sect</u> and <u>cult formation</u> as a response to the <u>decline</u> of the <u>dominant religious organizations</u>. <u>Similar</u> findings have been <u>reported in Europe</u>, thus further <u>strengthening this cyclical theory</u>.

Key Concepts

You should be able to explain the following concepts and be prepared to cite several examples of each concept.

Questions about ultimate meaning 352	Secularization 360
	Revival 360
Religion 354	Innovation (cult formation)
Supernatural 354	363
Religious economy 355	Cult 363
Religious pluralism 356	Charisma 364
Church 357	Unchurched belt 366
Sect 357	

Key Research Studies

You should be familiar with both the methodology and the results of the research studies cited here.

> Stark, Bainbridge, and others: relationship between church membership and various forms of deviation; application of church-sect theory to the concept of a religious economy; studies of rates of church membership, religious affiliation, and cult formation (throughout chapter)

Key Figures

Be able to associate each person with his contribution.

> H. Richard Niebuhr: church-sect theory
> Max Weber: concepts of church, sect, and charisma
> Benton Johnson: modification of church-sect theory

Key Theories

Be able to explain the assumptions of these theories and, when applicable, cite related research findings.

> Church-sect theory
> Religious economy

Completion

1. The marketplace of competing faiths within a society is termed a(n) _____.

2. All religions involve answers to questions about _____.

3. Religion entails socially organized patterns of beliefs and practices concerning ultimate meaning and assume the existence of the _____.

4. The natural state of a(n) _____ is religious pluralism.

5. _____ first distinguished between churches and sects.

6. _____ intellectualize religious teachings and restrain emotionalism in their services.

7. Sects stress _____ and individual mystic experience and tend toward _____.

8. Niebuhr argued that _____ provide for the religious needs of persons low in the stratification system.

9. Johnson suggested that church and sect are opposite poles on an axis representing the degree of tension between religious organizations and their _____.

10. Churches are religious bodies with relatively _____ tension whereas sects are religious bodies with relatively _____ tension.

11. A turning away from religious to secular explanations of life is termed _____.

12. The process of the formation of sects is called _____.

13. Revival is often a response to _____.

14. A religious movement that represents a new and unconventional faith is termed a(n) _____.

15. Weber termed the ability of some people to inspire faith in others _____.

16. Membership in conventional religious groups will be highest where _____ are most active.

17. In Canada and the United States, church membership is lowest in the _____.

18. In both the United States and Canada, approximately _____ of the population are church members.

19. Studies have found that _____ abound in places where church attendance is lowest.

20. _____ do best when they tap into a strong religious tradition, whereas _____ abound where the conventional religious tradition is weak.

Multiple Choice

1. Most sociologists agree that religion always entails:
   a. answers to questions of ultimate meaning
   b. the existence of the supernatural
   c. the belief in one supreme deity
   d. a and b
   e. all of the above

2. Religious institutions:
   a. can be a major force in holding societies together
   b. can give legitimacy and reason to the norms
   c. can give divine sanctions to the other institutions
   d. a and b
   e. all of the above

3. The natural state of a religious economy is:
   a. pluralism
   b. oligarchy
   c. monopoly
   d. monarchy
   e. anarchy

4. Churches:
   a. intellectualize religious teachings
   b. stress emotionalism
   c. tend toward fundamentalism in their teachings
   d. b and c
   e. all of the above

5. Sects:
   a. represent the gods as close at hand
   b. stress individual mystical experiences
   c. restrain emotionalism in their services
   d. a and b
   e. all of the above

6. Niebuhr argued that sects provide for the religious needs of people:
   a. of low status
   b. in the middle class
   c. in the upper class
   d. with high educational levels
   e. b and c

7. Johnson argued that _____ are religious bodies with relatively high tension.
   a. cults
   b. sects
   c. churches
   d. a and b
   e. all of the above

8. Traditionally, many social scientists believed that secularization would:
   a. lead to the eventual disappearance of religion
   b. increase membership in churches rather than sects
   c. foster the rise of cults
   d. increase membership in sects
   e. c and d

9. The formation of sects is termed:
   a. revelation
   b. revival
   c. secularization
   d. pluralism
   e. innovation

10. Responses to secularization include:
    a. revival
    b. cult formation
    c. religious change
    d. a and b
    e. all of the above

11. Sects are:
    a. new religions
    b. based on religions outside the conventional religious tradition
    c. new organizations reviving an old religion
    d. a and b
    e. none of the above

12. For <u>contemporary</u> sociologists of religion, the basis of charisma is:
    a. the ability to inspire faith in others
    b. the ability to get others to believe one's message
    c. the unusual ability to form attachments with others
    d. a and b
    e. none of the above

13. Research has found that almost _____ of North Americans are official members of a local congregation.
    a. four-fifths
    b. three-quarters
    c. two-thirds
    d. one-half
    e. one-third

14. Sect movements are clustered in those states where:
    a. membership in Christian churches is low
    b. membership in Christian churches is high
    c. church attendance is low
    d. a and c
    e. none of the above

15. In the United States, the "unchurched belt" is located in:
    a. the Deep South
    b. the Far West
    c. the Northeast
    d. the Middle West
    e. none of the above

16. Religious innovation in the United States is more common and successful in _____ than elsewhere in the nation.
    a. the Deep South
    b. the Far West
    c. the Northeast
    d. the Middle West
    e. New England

17. Which of the following statements is/are true?
    a. People who claim no religious affiliation are primarily nonbelievers.
    b. People who say they have no religion are least likely to express faith in unconventional supernatural beliefs.
    c. Cults abound in areas where church attendance is highest.
    d. all of the above
    e. none of the above

18. In contrast to the United States, the Canadian religious economy:
    a. is characterized by low church membership
    b. is more diverse than that of the United States
    c. is less diverse than that of the United States
    d. has experienced a decline in sectlike groups and a growth in denominations
    e. none of the above

19. The thesis that secularization is a self-limiting process that prompts revival and cult formation:
    a. has not been supported by data from Europe
    b. has not been supported by data from Canada
    c. has been supported by data from Europe and North America
    d. has been abandoned by contemporary sociologists
    e. none of the above

20. Today the average cult convert is likely to be:
    a. unusually well educated with excellent career potential
    b. poorly educated
    c. a social outcast
    d. b and c
    e. none of the above

_____
Essay

1. A. Define religion. (knowledge)
   B. Discuss the nature of religion. (comprehension)
   C. Contrast religion with other belief systems. (analysis)

2. A. Define a religious economy. (knowledge)
   B. Explain the following statement: "The natural state of a religious eonomy is pluralism." (comprehension)
   C. Apply the concept of a religious economy to the United States and Canada. (application)

3. Explain Niebuhr's church-sect theory. Discuss the later modifications of this theory.

4. How does the process of secularization lead to sect and cult formation?

5. Distinguish between a sect and cult. Discuss two research findings about geographical concentrations of sects and cults.

_____
Answers

Completion

1.	religious economy	11.	secularization
2.	ultimate meaning	12.	revival
3.	supernatural	13.	secularization
4.	religious economy	14.	cult
5.	Max Weber	15.	charisma
6.	Churches	16.	sects
7.	emotionalism, fundamentalism	17.	Far West (Pacific coast)
8.	sects	18.	two-thirds
9.	sociocultural environment	19.	cults
10.	low, high	20.	Sects, cults

Multiple Choice

1.	d	11.	c
2.	e	12.	c
3.	a	13.	c
4.	a	14.	b
5.	d	15.	b
6.	a	16.	b
7.	b	17.	e
8.	a	18.	c
9.	b	19.	c
10.	e	20.	a

CHAPTER 14
Politics and the State

Overview

Chapter 14 begins with a discussion of the preindustrial practice of the freedom of the commons and traces how population changes led to the tragedy of the commons. It then discusses the concept of collective goods and describes the functions of the state. It traces the rise of the repressive state and describes efforts in both England and the United States to tame the state. It looks at elitist and pluralist states and focuses upon Mills's concept of the power elite. The chapter then turns its attention to public opinion and focuses upon the Gallup Poll. Research on women candidates and voter preference is included among the "over-the-shoulder" examples. The chapter closes with a discussion of ideology and its role in political behavior.

Capsule Summary

States function to preserve internal order, maintain external security, and provide for collective goods. While some people have argued in favor of anarchy, most feel that the state is a necessary aspect of complex society. Since states use coercion, taming the state--that is, limiting its powers--has been a dominant historical issue. British and American history contain numerous examples of this process, which entails the establishment of both a clear set of rules defining the limits of power and a structure designed to ensure that the rules are observed.
    States are of two essential types: elitist and pluralist. Elitist states that are characterized by the rule of a single elite (sometimes termed the power elite) are the most common type. Pluralist states, on the other hand, are composed of many elites competing for power. In such states, power is distributed among various shifting coalitions.
    Public opinion polls, notably the Gallup Poll, are key indicators of public opinion about political issues. They are used extensively today to tap information about voter preference. Recent research has focused on the relationship between gender and voter preference. While many have argued that female candidates may not be successful because of their gender, research by Hunter and Denton and by Ekstrand and Eckert has found that the relationship between gender and vote getting is spurious and other factors are influential in this pattern.
    Ideologies, theories about how societies should be run, do not enjoy the popular appeal in Canada and the United States that they do in Europe. Indeed, the results of panel studies have shown that Americans do not often maintain the same ideological conviction over time. Often political interest here takes the form of interest in a specific issue rather than an underlying ideology; the term issue public identifies groups actively

involved in a particular issue. Rather than being strongly
ideological, as their European counterparts are, successful
political parties in America are really coalitions of many
internal issue publics.

Key Concepts

You should be prepared to explain these concepts and be able to
cite several examples of each concept.

Freedom of the commons   376

Public goods (collective
   goods)   381

State   381

Anarchy   383

Pluralism   386

Tyranny of the minority
   387

Tyranny of the majority
   387

System of checks and
   balances   387

Elitist state   387

Pluralist state   388

Power elite   390

Representative government
   390

Ideology   400

Panel study   403

Issue public   403

Key Research Studies

Be familiar with both the methodology and the results of the
research studies cited here.

Messick and Wilke: laboratory re-creation of freedom of the
                   commons   379

Gallup Poll data on political participation   393

Hunter and Denton: gender and vote getting ability   396

Ekstrand and Eckert: gender and voting experiment   397

Wuthnow; Stark and Bainbridge: ideology and attitudes   399

Key Figures

You should be able to associate each person with his contribution.

Mancur Olsen: relationship between public goods and coercion

Thomas Hobbes: Leviathan

James Madison: tyranny of the minority; tyranny of the
               majority; system of checks and balances

Plato: concept of philosopher-king

C. Wright Mills: The Power Elite

George Gallup: opinion polls

Be prepared to explain the assumptions of these theories and, when applicable, cite related research findings.

    Pluralist theory
    Taming of the state (not literally a theory)

_____
Completion

1. Olsen argued that in order to create _____ or _____ goods, the interests of the individual and the interests of the group collide.

2. The _____ or _____ is the organized embodiment of political processes within a society.

3. Only through organized _____ can humans assure themselves of public goods.

4. The practice in preindustrial England of allowing tenants to use all uncultivated pasture lands was termed _____.

5. Thomas Hobbes, in his book _____, describes what life would be like in a condition of anarchy.

6. In order for people to live in groups, internal order must be maintained, protection must be secured from external dangers, and _____ must be provided.

7. Plato advocated the creation of _____, persons trained to be fair and restrained in their use of state power.

8. _____ occurs when political power is dispersed among groups with diverse interests.

9. The danger that a majority of citizens will use the machinery of representative government to exploit and abuse minorities is termed _____.

10. The system known as _____ ensures that within the three branches of government each branch has the power to nullify actions taken by the other two.

11. The _____ state is the most common type.

12. In a(n) _____ state, rules governing state power are maintained by the existence of many competing elites.

13. Mills argued that the United States is effectively ruled by a small set of influential people who hold the preponderance of power; he called them the _____.

14. Research by Hunter and Denton has found that the relationship between gender and getting votes is _____ .

15. In a(n) _____ study, the same sample of respondents is interviewed several times.

16. A connected set of strongly held beliefs based on a few abstract ideas is termed a(n) _____ .

17. Converse used the term _____ to identify those who take interest in and who participate at least as observers in discussions of an issue.

18. Successful parties are coalitions of many internal _____ .

19. Compared with Europe, political parties in the United States _____ very ideological.

20. The first successful effort to conduct a public opinion poll that correctly predicted the outcome of a presidential election was led by _____ .

Multiple Choice

1. In order for a group to survive:
   a. internal order must be maintained
   b. it must be secure from external dangers
   c. public goods must be provided
   d. a and b
   e. all of the above

2. Research by Messick and Wilke (freedom of the commons simulation) found that:
   a. the subjects tended to use their power to exploit others
   b. the subjects behaved markedly different from the English lords
   c. the leaders in the experiment gave themselves smaller shares than they gave others
   d. all of the above
   e. none of the above

3. Public goods are vital because:
   a. we can't risk living together if we constantly fear for our lives and possessions
   b. certain resources and services must be provided that cannot be supplied by voluntary individual actions
   c. we must be secure from harm from other societies
   d. a and c
   e. all of the above

4. As societies become more complex:
   a. the machinery of state becomes less elaborate but more specialized
   b. the machinery of state becomes less elaborate and less specialized
   c. the machinery of state becomes more elaborate and more specialized
   d. fewer people hold positions as full-time leaders
   e. none of the above

5. In a condition of _____, political power is dispersed among groups with diverse interests.
   a. monarchy
   b. pluralism
   c. anarchy
   d. authoritarian rule
   e. communalism

6. _____ theory of the state holds that private property is the root of all repression and exploitation by the ruling class.
   a. Marxist
   b. Pluralist
   c. Anarchist
   d. Functionalist
   e. Weberian

7. Madison termed the danger that a privileged few would use the machinery of representative government to exploit and abuse the many:
   a. tyranny of the majority
   b. tyranny of the minority
   c. anarchy
   d. pluralist tyranny
   e. none of the above

8. In a pluralist state:
   a. rules governing state power are maintained by many competing elites
   b. all persons living in the state have an equal amount of power in decision making
   c. shifting coalitions of many minorities rule
   d. a and c
   e. none of the above

9. According to Mills, the power elite in the United States is mainly:
   a. Protestant
   b. male
   c. educated in Ivy League schools
   d. a and c
   e. all of the above

10. The rise of opinion polling is most closely associated with:
    a. Thomas Hobbes
    b. George Gallup
    c. C. Wright Mills
    d. Thomas Jefferson
    e. David Riesman

11. According to research by Hunter and Denton (gender and vote getting):
    a. political parties start losing because they nominate women
    b. after political parties start losing, they increase their rate of female nominations
    c. the effect of gender on vote getting may be spurious
    d. b and c
    e. all of the above

12. Research by Ekstrand and Eckert (experiment in gender and voting) has shown that:
    a. the gender of the candidate did not seem to matter
    b. the gender of the student subject had a strong effect on that subject's preference
    c. the students strongly favored conservative candidates
    d. b and c
    e. all of the above

13. An ideology:
    a. is a connected set of strongly held beliefs based on a few abstract ideas
    b. is used to guide one's reaction to external events
    c. is essentially a theory about life
    d. b and c
    e. all of the above

14. A study in which the same sample of respondents is interviewed several times is termed a(n) _____ study.
    a. retrospective
    b. case
    c. panel
    d. ex post facto
    e. none of the above

15. Converse used the term _____ to identify those who take an interest in and who participate at least as observers in discussions of an issue.
    a. interest groups
    b. ideology supporters
    c. interest publics
    d. issue publics
    e. support groups

16. Many people lack political ideologies because:
    a. people rarely invent their own
    b. ideologies are intellectual creations often involving many different authors and interpreters
    c. only elites can create and preserve ideologies
    d. all of the above
    e. none of the above

17. In the United States and Canada, successful political parties:
    a. are strongly ideological
    b. appeal to a narrow interest group within an electorate
    c. are coalitions of many internal issue publics
    d. a and b
    e. none of the above

18. The taming of the state requires that:
    a. a clear set of rules must be established that define the limits of state power
    b. a clear set of rules must be established that define how the state's power can and cannot be exercised
    c. a structure must be set up in which power is widely dispersed among many powerful groups
    d. a and b
    e. all of the above

19. Elitist states:
    a. are nonexistent today
    b. never call themselves democracies
    c. are the most common type of government
    d. b and c
    e. none of the above

20. Who of the following is not correctly paired with his contribution?
    a. Thomas Hobbes: Leviathan
    b. James Madison: system of checks and balances
    c. George Gallup: the desirability of anarchy
    d. Plato: concept of philosopher-king
    e. C. Wright Mills: The Power Elite

_____
Essay

1. A. Name the two types of states. (knowledge)
   B. Give examples of these two types of states. (comprehension)
   C. Contrast elitist states with pluralist states. (analysis)

2. A. Name three functions of the state. (knowledge)
    B. Explain Olsen's argument about the necessity of coercion.
        (comprehension)
    C. Apply his argument to the taming of the state.
        (application)

3. Trace the taming of the state in England and the United
    States.

4. What is a political ideology? Compare and contrast political
    and religious ideologies. Explain the following statement:
    "Compared with Europe, politics in the United States is not
    very ideological."

5. Explain the following statement: "Election day results do
    not mirror public opinion."

_____

Answers

Completion

1.   public, collective   11. elitist
2.   state, government   12. pluralist
3.   coercion   13. power elite
4.   freedom of the commons   14. spurious
5.   Leviathan   15. panel
6.   public (collective)   16. ideology
       goods   17. issue publics
7.   philosopher-kings   18. issue publics
8.   Pluralism   19. are not
9.   tyranny of the majority   20. Gallup
10. checks and balances

Multiple Choice

1.   e   11. d
2.   a   12. a
3.   e   13. e
4.   c   14. c
5.   b   15. d
6.   a   16. d
7.   b   17. c
8.   d   18. e
9.   e   19. c
10. b   20. c

CHAPTER 15
The Interplay Between Education and Occupation

Overview

After opening with a discussion of the interplay between education
and occupation, this chapter discusses the prestige rankings of
occupations. It examines the changing nature of work and the
composition of the labor force. Chapter 15 discusses unemployment
and focuses on the relationship between the changing nature of
work and rates of unemployment. It then considers the history of
education in America and the current concern with the decline in
the quality of education; the issue of the importance of schools
and the related research of Coleman and Heyns are discussed. The
chapter closes with an in-depth discussion of Meyer's theory of
educational functions.

Capsule Summary

The interplay of education and occupation is a dominant feature of
societies. Education has always been highly valued in America.
Its importance has increased as we have moved from primarily an
industrial economy to a knowledge economy. Typically those whose
educational level is high enjoy not only greater income but also
greater prestige; a person's occupation is a major source of
prestige. Prestige rankings, which tend to be relatively
consistent over time and place, have shown that the more training
or skill required for an occupation, the higher its prestige.
     During this century the nature of work and of education have
changed. More positions require skill and extensive training and
fewer rely on physical labor. Hence, unemployment rates for the
unskilled are high. Women have entered the work force in greater
numbers, partly as a response to the change in the nature of work.
More students are staying in school longer; high school graduation
is commonplace and the majority of Americans enter college. With
the increase in the number of people becoming better educated,
there has been concern that the quality of education has
diminished. Evidence from declining Scholastic Achievement Test
(SAT) scores seems to support that claim.
     Research has focused on the functions of schools. People
have long assumed that the quality of a school would have an effect
on learning. Coleman's study, however, found that school quality
had no detectable impact on student achievement scores.
     Heyns found that summer vacation seemed to be most
detrimental to lower-income children, who probably benefit the
most from school. Further research by Alexander and others and by
Heyneman and Loxley has produced further evidence of the
importance of education for the disadvantaged. There has been
recent concern with the "devaluation of education." Meyer's
theory of educational functions argues for the importance of

education as a socializing agent. He concludes that the main
function of education is to confer prestigious statuses and to
train persons to play the roles attached to them. Similarly,
colleges have the power to create new positions that are accorded
high prestige. For people with such status, the prestige and
life-style associated with it do not end upon graduation but
rather become a lifelong identity.

Key Concepts

You should be ready to explain the concepts listed here, as well
as be able to give several examples of each concept.

Occupational prestige   408   Unemployment   414
Scientific management   411   Educational "deflation"   424
Knowledge economy   411

Key Research Studies

You should be familiar with both the methodology and the results
of the following research studies.

Taylor: time and motion studies of work   410
Hatt and North: occupational prestige rankings in the United
States   408
Pineo and Porter: occupational prestige rankings in Canada
408
Coleman: quality of schools and student achievement scores
419
Heyns: the effects of summer vacation on learning   420
Alexander, Natriello, and Pallas: cognitive development of
high school students and
dropouts   421
Heyneman and Loxley: school effects worldwide   423

Key Theories

Know how to explain the assumptions of these theories and, when
applicable, cite related research findings.

Allocation theories
Meyer's theory of educational functions

The following are not exactly theories per se, but knowledge of
these trends and changes is essential for understanding this
chapter.

Higher education in twentieth-century America
Changes in the composition of the work force

Completion

1. Generally the more education people have, the _____ they earn and the _____ their occupational status.

2. The more training an occupation requires and the more pay it offers, the _____ its public prestige.

3. The application of scientific techniques to improve work efficiency is termed _____.

4. Technological innovations have made it possible to work _____.

5. According to Drucker, we are changing from a primarily industrial economy to a(n) _____ economy.

6. The term _____ is applied to those 16 years old and older who are without jobs and are seeking work.

7. Coleman found that school quality had little impact on student _____.

8. Collins argued that education was not meant to prepare people for careers but to protect _____.

9. Heyns found that schools greatly improve the education of _____ children.

10. Heyns found that the single activity most strongly and consistently related to summer learning is _____.

11. Research by Alexander and others found that dropping out of high school had the most severe negative effects on students from the most _____ backgrounds.

12. The _____ the nation, the greater the economic returns for getting an education.

13. As the level of education has risen in industrial nations, the relative advantage of completing a given level of education has _____.

14. Meyer argued that variations in school quality seem of _____ importance in the attitudes, values, opinions, and behaviors of graduates.

15. Meyer argued that the real impact of schools is to admit people to a particular _____.

16. _____ theories argue that education is a passive servant of the stratification system.

132

17. Meyer argued that education helps create new classes of
    _____ and _____, which then come to be incorporated
    into society.

18. As more people get an education, a given level of education
    becomes _____ valuable.

19. The respect given to people on the basis of their jobs is
    termed _____.

20. Those persons who are employed or seeking employment make up
    the _____.

Multiple Choice

1. Studies of occupational prestige:
   a. yield results that are fairly stable over time and place
   b. have shown that many of the higher prestige positions
      require a college education
   c. have found that Canadians have a markedly different
      ranking system than Americans
   d. a and b
   e. b and c

2. The interplay between education and occupation:
   a. begins in adolescence
   b. begins early in life
   c. does not manifest itself until adulthood
   d. is declining as a result of "working smarter"
   e. none of the above

3. Drucker has argued that:
   a. modern workers work harder and smarter than their
      grandparents did
   b. we are changing from a primarily industrial economy to a
      knowledge economy
   c. we are changing from a knowledge economy to an industrial
      economy
   d. a and b
   e. none of the above

4. Reasons for the increased participation of women in the work
   force include:
   a. the feminist movement
   b. reduced fertility
   c. a change in the kinds of work available
   d. a and b
   e. all of the above

5. The labor force has expanded because:
   a. a greater proportion of young people are working today
   b. a greater proportion of older people are working today
   c. women have entered the work force
   d. a and c
   e. all of the above

6. The term <u>unemployed</u> includes only:
   a. those 16 and older
   b. those without jobs
   c. those who are seeking work
   d. a and b
   e. all of the above

7. Reasons for the high rates of unemployment among blacks include:
   a. discrimination
   b. the fact that blacks today are far less likely to enter college than whites
   c. the dwindling supply of unskilled labor jobs
   d. a and c
   e. all of the above

8. Coleman's study found that:
   a. school quality had a major impact on student achievement scores
   b. teachers' educational levels have a major impact on student achievement scores
   c. school quality did not have a major impact on student achievement scores
   d. summer vacation had little effect on students' achievement
   e. a and b

9. Today approximately _____ of Americans are in the labor force.
   a. 64 percent
   b. 75 percent
   c. 40 percent
   d. 88 percent
   e. 51 percent

10. A major reason for the decline in the intellectual quality of teachers is that:
   a. more women are becoming teachers
   b. minorities are increasingly entering the teaching profession
   c. changing sex roles are allowing highly talented women to enter professions other than teaching
   d. the proportion of teachers who are male is increasing
   e. none of the above

11. Heyns found that schools:
    a. merely maintain the differences that poor and middle-class children bring to schools
    b. greatly improve the education of poor children
    c. greatly improve the education of middle-class children but have little effect on poor children
    d. have little effect on either poor or middle-class children
    e. none of the above

12. Heyns's study of the effect of summer vacation found that:
    a. attending summer school prevents learning losses during summer
    b. children from all levels were harmed by summer vacations
    c. children from higher-income families learned about as much during vacation as they did during the school year
    d. a and b
    e. none of the above

13. Research by Heyneman and Loxley on school effects in 29 nations found that:
    a. the poorer the nation, the less that students' backgrounds influence their school performances
    b. children in less industrialized nations learn more during the same number of school years than those in more industrialized nations
    c. the poorer the nation, the less the economic returns for getting an education
    d. a and b
    e. all of the above

14. The decline of the value of a college education can be attributed to:
    a. the result of colleges not preparing people for careers
    b. the rising relative earnings of blue-collar workers, which have surpassed the earnings of some college graduates
    c. the fact that college graduates are no longer a scarce commodity
    d. b and c
    e. all of the above

15. Meyer argued that:
    a. a major effect of education is that people learn to play the role appropriate to the status that their school confers on them
    b. the most powerful socializing property of schools is the ability to confer statuses that are recognized in the society at large
    c. educational institutions have the power to create new occupations and to control the placement of these occupations in the occupational structure
    d. all of the above
    e. none of the above

16. Allocation theorists argue that the primary purpose of education is to:
    a. place people in a particular status
    b. educate children
    c. serve as a passive servant of the stratification system
    d. a and c
    e. none of the above

17. _____ made an early attempt to apply scientific techniques to increase efficiency (scientific management).
    a. Frederick W. Taylor
    b. James Coleman
    c. Barbara Heyns
    d. Paul Hatt and Cecil North
    e. Ivan Illich

18. The term <u>unemployed</u> does <u>not</u> include persons who:
    a. are enrolled in school
    b. are not of legal working age
    c. are not actively seeking a job
    d. b and c
    e. all of the above

19. Today women make up slightly over _____ of the labor force in Canada and the United States.
    a. 25 percent
    b. 40 percent
    c. 55 percent
    d. 68 percent
    e. 75 percent

20. Long-term unemployment tends to be concentrated in:
    a. the Appalachia region of the United States
    b. the Pacific region of Canada and the United States
    c. minorities
    d. a and c
    e. all of the above

Essay

1. A. Name two functions of schools. (knowledge)
   B. Discuss Meyer's theory of educational functions. (comprehension)
   C. Contrast Meyer's theory with allocation theories. (analysis)

2. A. Explain the concept of a knowledge economy. (comprehension)
   B. Show the interplay of education and occupation in a knowledge economy. (application)
   C. Contrast an industrial economy with a knowledge economy. (analysis)

3. Trace the history of American higher education in the twentieth century.

4. Discuss some of the findings of either Coleman's study or Heyns's study.

5. Discuss some of the reasons why the quality of education seems to have declined in recent years.

Answers

Completion

1.	more, higher	11.	disadvantaged
2.	greater	12.	poorer
3.	scientific management	13.	declined
4.	smarter	14.	little or no
5.	knowledge	15.	educational status
6.	unemployed	16.	Allocation
7.	achievement	17.	knowledge, personnel
8.	class interests	18.	less
9.	poor	19.	occupational prestige
10.	reading	20.	labor force

Multiple Choice

1.	d	11.	b
2.	b	12.	c
3.	b	13.	a
4.	e	14.	d
5.	c	15.	e
6.	e	16.	d
7.	d	17.	a
8.	c	18.	e
9.	a	19.	b
10.	c	20.	d

CHAPTERS 12 TO 15
Review and Special Project

This section focused upon the major social institutions: the family, religion, the political order, the economy, and education. It discussed not only the nature of these institutions but also emphasized changes in them.

Special Project

You might wish to investigate a specific change that you believe has occurred in one of these institutions during the past few decades. Possible topics for investigation might include the following:

1. The increase in the number of one-parent homes.
2. The change in the divorce rate of a particular category of persons (families with young children, people over 50, and so on).
3. The increase (or decrease) in church attendance or membership in a specific denomination or sect.
4. The increase (or decrease) in political participation (voting rates, registration rates) of a particular group (persons under 30, blacks, and so on).
5. The increase (or decrease) in the number of women in a particular profession.

To ascertain these changes you will need to obtain data from 1940 or 1950 and then compare these statistics with more recent ones. Sociologists often make use of the wealth of information available from Gallup Polls, census data, and government reports when studying trends and changes over time. Most of these statistics are readily available through your school or public library. (You may be surprised to see the wide variety of information that is available.) You will also want to investigate research journals for specific studies in your area of investigation. The Sociological Abstracts, an index of articles published in major journals, is of great assistance in locating relevant articles.

Once you have obtained your data, you may want to further investigate these trends. You may wish to locate studies and theories that attempt to explain these changes within the context of general societal change.

CHAPTER 16
Social Change and Modernization

Overview

A discussion of modernization and sources of social change opens
Chapter 16. It explains cultural lag and highlights the Iranian
revolution as an example of this concept. It also describes
capitalism as an economic system and contrasts capitalism with
command economies. Chapter 16 then offers an in-depth discussion
of four theories of modernization: the Marxist view, Weber on
Protestantism and the emergence of capitalism, the state theory
of modernization, and the world system (dependency) theory. It
closes with an "over-the-shoulder" view of Delacroix's test of
the dependency hypothesis.

Capsule Summary

Modernization is the process by which agrarian societies are
transformed into industrial societies. Social systems undergo
change from both internal and external sources. Internal sources
of change include innovations, new technology, new culture, new
social structures, group conflict, and growth. External sources
include diffusion, conflict, and ecological change. Cultural lag
often occurs during times of social change.
    Despite their differences, all theories of modernization
attribute modernization in the West to capitalism. In contrast
to command economies, capitalism is characterized by private
ownership, competition for profits, and a free market.
Capitalism encourages an individual to produce as much as possible
because it rewards hard work and reinvestment of profits.
    Karl Marx attributed the Industrial Revolution to
capitalism. He believed that capitalism encouraged people to
work harder and develop ideas, thus fostering technological
advances. While he argued that capitalism was necessary for
modernization, he believed that by promoting self-interest,
capitalism fostered alienation, inequality, and class conflict.
Marx believed that once modernization was accomplished, communist
revolutions would foster collective ownership and allow the
benefits of modernization to be shared equally.
    Max Weber explained the emergence of capitalism as a result
of religious doctrines of the Protestant Reformation. He argued
that belief in predestination fostered an ideology that
encouraged production, thrift, and the reinvestment of profit.
Over time these values lost much of their religious significance
and became basic secular values that were congruent with the
economic system of capitalism.
    The state theory of modernization argues that both
capitalism and Protestantism are the result of the taming of the
state. Repressive societies are characterized by command

economies. As the power of the state is limited, people have
more chances to pursue economic self-interest; this in turn will
encourage technological progress and capitalism. This theory
argues that capitalism can only emerge once the state is tame.

In contrast to the preceding theories, world system
(dependency) theory looks to external sources of change. It
argues that in the world system, stratification exists among
nations. The dominant nations, termed core nations by
Wallerstein, exploit the weaker peripheral nations. Core nations
are highly modernized while modernization in peripheral nations
is hampered by this domination. In his test of the dependency
hypothesis, Delacroix did not find support for the assumptions of
this theory.

Key Concepts

You should be able to explain the concepts listed here; you
should also be able to give several examples of each concept.

Modernization 433	Command economies 443
Innovation 434	Empire 448
Cultural lag 437	Core nations 448
Social evolution 439	Peripheral nations 448
Diffusion 439	Semiperipheral nations 449
Capitalism 443	Dependency hypothesis 452

Key Research Study

Be familiar with both the methodology and the results of the
following study.

Delacroix: test of the dependency hypothesis   452

Key Figures

You should be able to associate each person with his
contribution.

William Ogburn: concept of cultural lag
Max Weber: The Protestant Ethic and the Spirit of Capitalism
Martin Luther: Protestant Reformation
John Calvin: doctrine of predestination

Key Theories

Be prepared to explain the assumptions of these theories of modernization and, when applicable, cite related research findings.

> Karl Marx: capitalism
> Max Weber: the Protestant Ethic and the emergence of capitalism
> State theory of modernization
> World system (dependency) theory

Completion

1. The process by which agrarian societies are transformed into industrial societies is termed _____.

2. Diffusion is the transfer of _____.

3. Types of innovation that may cause social change include new technology, new culture, and new _____.

4. The delay between the change in one part of society that produces a realignment of the other parts may cause _____.

5. The concept of cultural lag is associated with _____.

6. External sources of change include diffusion, conflict, and _____.

7. An economic system that is based on private ownership of the means of production and relies on a free market is called _____.

8. A unique feature of _____ is that it relies on a free market.

9. Economies in which some people decide what work is to be done and order others to do it are termed _____.

10. The secret of capitalism is to reward _____.

11. _____ argued that the religious ideas produced by Protestantism motivated people to limit their consumption and pursue maximum wealth.

12. The state theory of modernization argues that _____ will always develop when the state is tame.

13. Chirot argued that the untamed state is incapable of not stifling economic development because it is incapable of not _____.

14. The doctrine of predestination is associated with _____.

15. _____ states that exploitation among nations promotes modernization in some countries and hinders it in others.

16. Wallerstein argued that within the world system _____ exists among nations.

17. _____ nations have highly specialized economies, weak internal political structures, and a low standard of living for workers.

18. Wallerstein termed the dominant nations in the world system _____ nations.

19. Delacroix argued that modernization is influenced primarily by _____ processes.

20. The first effect of modernization on the less developed nations has been an immense _____ in recent decades.

_____

Multiple Choice

1. Internal sources of social change include:
   a. innovations
   b. group conflicts
   c. growth
   d. a and c
   e. all of the above

2. New technology:
   a. may appear and go unused for a long time
   b. changes societies by itself
   c. can be a major source of social change
   d. a and c
   e. all of the above

3. Innovation may result in:
   a. new technology
   b. new culture
   c. new social structures
   d. a and c
   e. all of the above

4. The period of delay between the time one part of society changes and the other parts realign is termed:
    a. diffusion delay
    b. cultural lag
    c. innovation lag
    d. cultural discontinuation
    e. none of the above

5. The term cultural lag is associated with:
    a. Max Weber
    b. Karl Marx
    c. William Ogburn
    d. John Calvin
    e. Immanuel Wallerstein

6. The transfer of innovations is termed:
    a. cultural lag
    b. diffusion
    c. accommodation
    d. social evolution
    e. assimilation

7. External sources of social change include:
    a. diffusion
    b. conflict
    c. changes in the physical environment
    d. a and b
    e. all of the above

8. An economic system based on private ownership of the means of production and a system by which people compete to gain profits is termed:
    a. capitalism
    b. communism
    c. socialism
    d. privateering
    e. command economy

9. Capitalism is unique in its:
    a. economic system based on private ownership of the means of production
    b. emphasis on competition to gain profits
    c. reliance on a free market
    d. emphasis on communal goods
    e. a and b

10. Command economies:
    a. rely on free market principles
    b. reward surplus production
    c. encourage consumption
    d. a and b
    e. all of the above

11. Capitalistic economies:
    a. rely on a free market
    b. encourage immediate consumption
    c. reward surplus production
    d. a and c
    e. all of the above

12. The doctrine of predestination is associated with:
    a. Martin Luther
    b. Karl Marx
    c. John Calvin
    d. Immanuel Wallerstein
    e. none of the above

13. Weber argued that capitalism:
    a. blossomed from its roots in the Protestant Ethic
    b. became a secular ideology in its own right
    c. was caused solely by the Protestant Ethic
    d. a and b
    e. all of the above

14. The state theory of modernization argues that:
    a. capitalism will develop when the state is tame
    b. Protestant theology led to the development of capitalism
    c. modernization is the result of changes introduced from other societies
    d. a and c
    e. all of the above

15. Theories that seek the causes of the Industrial Revolution within societies include:
    a. world system theory
    b. Marxist theory
    c. dependency theory
    d. a and c
    e. b and c

16. According to world system theory, core nations:
    a. have weak or unstable governments
    b. have a low standard of living for workers
    c. have highly diversified economies
    d. b and c
    e. all of the above

17. In his test of the dependence hypothesis, Delacroix found that:
    a. nations specializing in raw material exports showed an increase in per capita GNP equal to that of nations specializing in the export of manufactured goods
    b. modernization is influenced by external processes of the world system
    c. extensive support exists for the dependency hypothesis
    d. all of the above
    e. none of the above

18. According to world system theory:
    a. stratification exists among nations
    b. the class position of a nation is determined by its place in a geographical division of labor
    c. less developed nations are economically dominated by more developed ones
    d. all of the above
    e. none of the above

19. Who of the following is/are <u>not</u> correctly paired with his theory or contribution?
    a. William Ogburn: cultural lag
    b. Immanuel Wallerstein: state theory of modernization
    c. John Calvin: predestination
    d. Martin Luther: Protestant Reformation
    e. a and b

20. _____ wrote <u>The Protestant Ethic and the Spirit of Capitalism</u>.
    a. John Calvin
    b. Martin Luther
    c. Max Weber
    d. Karl Marx
    e. Immanuel Wallerstein

<u>Essay</u>

1. A. Name the four theories of modernization. (knowledge)
   B. Explain two of these theories. (comprehension)
   C. Compare and contrast two of these theories. (analysis)

2. A. Define cultural lag. (knowledge)
   B. Give several examples of cultural lag. (comprehension)
   C. Apply this concept to the Iranian Revolution. (application)

3. Discuss some internal and external sources of social change; give an example of each.

4. Explain Weber's theory of the relationship between the Protestant Ethic and the emergence of capitalism.

5. Explain world system theory and show how Delacroix's study did not support the dependency hypothesis.

Answers

Completion

1. modernization
2. innovations
3. social structures
4. cultural lag
5. William Ogburn
6. stratification
7. capitalism
8. capitalism
9. command economies
10. surplus production
11. Max Weber
12. capitalism
13. overtaxing
14. John Calvin
15. World system theory
16. stratification
17. Peripheral
18. core
19. internal
20. population explosion

Multiple Choice

1. e
2. d
3. e
4. b
5. c
6. b
7. e
8. a
9. c
10. c
11. d
12. c
13. d
14. a
15. b
16. c
17. a
18. d
19. b
20. c

CHAPTER 17
Population Changes

A discussion of demography and early uses of government census opens Chapter 17. The chapter then focuses upon the various rates and measures used by contemporary demographers. After examining preindustrial population trends and Malthusian theory, it discusses population changes resulting from modernization and focuses on the theory of demographic transition. Chapter 17 looks at the second population explosion and recent research by Berelson and by Cutright and Smith on the fertility decline in developing nations. A special topic section devoted to changes in society caused by the "baby boom" follows the chapter.

Capsule Summary

Demography is the study of population. Demographers study not only population size but also population changes and trends. Although demographic theory has its roots in the work of Adam Smith, governments throughout history have often conducted a census (such as the Domesday Book) for tax purposes. Demographers today often use extensive measures such as crude rates, specific rates, cohorts, and age and sex structures to measure population trends and provide a basis for long-term planning.

Early societies often had a difficult time maintaining their populations. The first major increase in population occurred with the development of agriculture. Agricultural societies can produce more food and hence support greater numbers, but they are vulnerable to famines and disease, which reduce their numbers. With the advent of modernization, a population explosion occurred as a result of both agricultural innovations and a marked decrease in the mortality rate.

Malthusian theory attempts to explain the periodic growth and decline of populations prior to modernization. It postulates that populations always grow to a size slightly above the available food supply. Positive checks such as disease and famine then reduce the population to a size congruent with the available food and the cycle begins again.

The theory of demographic transition attempts to explain the population growth associated with modernization. This transition involves a change from the long-established pattern of high fertility and high but variable mortality to one of low fertility and low mortality. It argues that while modernization markedly cuts the death rate, it also encourages decreased fertility as large families become a liability rather than an asset. Cultural lag may occur between the initial decline in the mortality rate and the corresponding decline in the birth rate, causing a temporary rapid increase in population. This has occurred in the past few decades in less developed countries, although recent research by <u>Berelson</u> and others has detected the beginning of a decline in fertility in some of these nations.

Key Concepts

You should be able to explain the following concepts, as well as be able to cite several examples of each concept.

<u>Domesday Book</u>   456
Census   458
Demography   458
Growth rate   459
Crude death rate   459
Crude birth rate   459
Fertility rate   460
Age-specific death
  rate   461
Birth cohort   461
Age structure   463

Sex structure 463
Expansive population structure
  463
Stationary populaton structure
  464
Constrictive population structure
  464
Positive checks   469
Replacement-level fertility   472
Zero population growth   473

Key Research Studies

You should be familiar with both the methodology and the results of the research studies cited here.

Berelson: thresholds of modernization--fertility reduction
          among less developed nations   474
Cutright and Smith: population patterns of less developed
          nations   481

Key Figures

Be able to associate each person with his contribution.

William the Conqueror: <u>Domesday Book</u>
Adam Smith: foundations of demographic theory
Thomas R. Malthus: <u>Essay on the Principles of Population</u>
Kingsley Davis: theory of demographic transition
Paul Ehrlich: <u>The Population Bomb</u>

_____
Key Theories

You should be prepared to explain the assumptions of these
theories and, when applicable, cite related research findings.

   Malthusian theory
   Theory of demographic transition

_____
Completion

1.   A population count is termed a(n) _____.

2.   Demography is the study of _____.

3.   The net population gain (or loss) divided by the size of
     the population constitutes the _____.

4.   The _____ can be computed by dividing the total number
     of deaths for a year by the total population for that year.

5.   The total number of births divided by the total number of
     females within a certain age span is termed the _____.

6.   All persons born within a given time period such as a year
     constitute the _____.

7.   An expansive population structure is characteristic of
     present populations in _____ nations.

8.   A declining population reflects a(n) _____ population
     structure.

9.   The first great shift in population trends was caused by the
     development of _____.

10. Sudden rises in mortality rates in primitive societies can
     be the result of war, _____, and _____.

11. _____ wrote An Essay on the Principles of Population.

12. Malthus called famine, disease, and war _____.

13. The second great shift in population was caused by the
     _____.

14. _____ fertility occurs when the number of births each
     year equals the number of deaths.

15. The theory of demographic transition is closely associated
     with _____.

16. As a result of modernization, children ceased to be a(n)
 _____ and became a(n) _____.

17. The fourth great shift in population trends was massive,
 unprecedented population growth in _____.

18. Cutright and Smith argued that until a life expectancy of 46
 years is reached, there is no correlation between life
 expectancy and _____.

19. The proportion of males and females in a population is
 termed the _____.

20. The medieval census conducted by William the Conquerer
 following his takeover of England was termed the _____
 Book.

Multiple Choice

1. The study of population is termed:
 a. ecology
 b. ethnology
 c. democracy
 d. demography
 e. none of the above

2. A population can decline because:
 a. births are increasing
 b. deaths are increasing
 c. people are migrating into a region
 d. a and c
 e. all of the above

3. The number of deaths in a year divided by the total
 population for that year is termed the:
 a. crude death rate
 b. mortality rate
 c. age-specific death rate
 d. growth rate
 e. death cohort

4. All of the persons born in a given time period constitute
 the:
 a. crude birth rate
 b. age-specific birth rate
 c. fertility rate
 d. growth rate
 e. birth cohort

5. An expansive population structure:
   a. reflects a declining population
   b. has fewer people on the bottom than in the middle
   c. is characteristic of underdeveloped nations
   d. a and b
   e. all of the above

6. A rapid increase in the death rate may be the result of:
   a. famine
   b. disease
   c. war
   d. all of the above
   e. none of the above

7. Which of the following has/have a positive effect on fertility?
   a. affluence
   b. religion
   c. the proportion of males in the population
   d. a and b
   e. all of the above

8. The first great shift in population trends was caused by:
   a. the modernization of agriculture
   b. the development of agriculture
   c. the decline in mortality due to better sanitation standards
   d. the introduction of technology
   e. none of the above

9. According to Malthus:
   a. population growth will tend to rise slightly above the supply of food
   b. fertility could be controlled through moral restraint
   c. both fertility and mortality periodically rise and fall
   d. a and c
   e. all of the above

10. According to Malthus, positive checks on population include:
    a. disease
    b. moral restraint
    c. war
    d. a and c
    e. all of the above

11. During the initial period of modernization:
    a. the industrialization of agriculture increased the food supply
    b. the population grew rapidly
    c. the mortality rate dropped markedly
    d. all of the above
    e. none of the above

12. Replacement-level fertility:
    a. occurs when the number of births each year equals the number of deaths
    b. produces zero population growth as soon as the age structure has adjusted
    c. has yet to be reached in industrialized nations
    d. a and b
    e. all of the above

13. The demographic transition involves:
    a. a change from high fertility to low fertility
    b. a change from low fertility to high fertility
    c. a change from low mortality to high mortality
    d. b and c
    e. none of the above

14. Davis argued that modernization encouraged low fertility because:
    a. the decline in infant and childhood mortality eliminated the need for families to have many children to ensure that some survived to adulthood
    b. large families became an asset rather than a burden
    c. birth control devices were invented early in the Industrial Revolution
    d. a and b
    e. all of the above

15. Thresholds of modernization include the characteristic(s) that:
    a. more than half of the labor force is not employed in agriculture
    b. 80 percent of the females age 15 to 19 are not married
    c. at least one half of the adults can read
    d. a and b
    e. all of the above

16. The second population explosion:
    a. occurred in Western nations
    b. occurred during the 1970s and early 1980s
    c. resulted from a rapid drop in the mortality rate
    d. a and b
    e. all of the above

17. By the early 1970s, demographers detected a _____ in the less developed nations.
    a. fertility increase
    b. fertility decline
    c. mortality increase
    d. mortality decline
    e. none of the above

18. The proportion of males and females in a population constitutes the:
    a. sex rate
    b. sex structure
    c. sex ratio
    d. fertility rate
    e. fertility ratio

19. An age structure in which younger cohorts are smaller than the ones before them is termed a(n) _____.
    a. stationary population structure
    b. constrictive population
    c. expansive population
    d. modernized population
    e. none of the above

20. Who of the following is not correctly paired with his contribution?
    a. Paul Ehrlich: Domesday Book
    b. Thomas Malthus: Essay on the Principles of Population
    c. Kingsley Davis: theory of demographic transition
    d. all of the above
    e. none of the above

Essay

1. A. Define demography. (knowledge)
   B. Explain Malthusian theory. (comprehension)
   C. Contrast Malthusian theory with the theory of demographic transition. (analysis)

2. A. Define the theory of demographic transition. (knowledge)
   B. Using the concept of cultural lag, explain the second population explosion and recent population trends in developing nations. (comprehension)
   C. Apply either the theory of demographic transition or Malthusian theory to the current situation in developing nations. (application)

3. Describe some of the population characteristics of preindustrial societies.

4. Discuss some of the changes that occurred during the first population explosion.

5. Discuss some of the changes that have occurred as a result of the "baby boom." (This question is drawn from Special Topic 6.)

Answers

Completion

1.	census	11.	Thomas Malthus
2.	population	12.	positive checks
3.	growth rate	13.	Industrial Revolution
			(or modernization of agriculture)
4.	crude death rate	14.	Replacement-level
5.	fertility rate	15.	Kingsley Davis
6.	birth cohort	16.	economic asset, economic burden
7.	underdeveloped	17.	less developed nations
8.	constrictive	18.	fertility
9.	agriculture	19.	sex structure
10.	disease, famine	20.	Domesday

Multiple Choice

1.	d	11.	d
2.	b	12.	e
3.	a	13.	a
4.	e	14.	a
5.	c	15.	e
6.	d	16.	c
7.	b	17.	b
8.	b	18.	b
9.	e	19.	b
10.	d	20.	a

CHAPTER 18
Urbanization

Overview

After opening with a description of preindustrial cities, this
chapter describes the impact of the agricultural revolution and
industrialization on urban growth. It introduces the concept of a
metropolis and distinguishes between the fixed-rail metropolis and
the freeway metropolis. Ethnic neighborhoods are then discussed,
highlighting both Park and Burgess's early theory and recent tests
of that theory. The chapter then examines the work of early
theorists such as Tönnies, Durkheim, and Wirth and cites relevant
research. Chapter 18 ends with a discussion of both the macro and
micro effects of crowding.

Capsule Summary

Urbanization, the migration from rural areas to cities, was the
result of modernization. Prior to the agricultural revolution and
industrialization, cities were small, dirty, disease-ridden, and
crowded. Despite these conditions, people did migrate to
preindustrial cities in search of economic gain, adventure, and
anonymity. The agricultural revolution made it possible for
larger numbers of people to live in the city; specialization also
required a large urban work force.
        Today the term city is rather nebulous. Since many people
live in suburbs surrounding a city, the term metropolis (or
metropolitan area) has come to refer to a city and its sphere of
influence. Modern cities have been shaped by transportation.
Older industrial cities are termed fixed-rail metropolises since
their growth followed the railroad lines outward from the center
of the city. More recently, the decentralized freeway metropolis
has emerged, and research indicates that people seem to prefer to
reside in such an area.
        Many cities contain ethnic and racial neighborhoods. The
ethnic populations of these areas change over time due to a
process termed succession. Park and Burgess argued that slum
neighborhoods are successively occupied by the lowest status
groups. Guest and Weed, using the index of dissimilarity,
recently found support for this theory and concluded that the
barriers to integration were economic rather than ethnic or
racial. Taeuber recently reported that American cities have
become less segregated as blacks have moved into the suburbs and
white neighborhoods.
        Early theorists took a negative view of the city. Tönnies's
contrast of Gemeinschaft and Gesellschaft portrayed Gesellschaft
relationships as cold and impersonal. Durkheim (and later Wirth)
argued that urban areas were characterized by high rates of anomie
and resulting deviance. However, recent research has failed to
support the assumption that anomie is characteristic of urbanites.

Researchers have studied both _macro_ and _micro_ effects of _crowding_. Studies have not found any significant differences in pathology rates between areas of high and low population density. On the other hand, research by _Gove_ and others found considerable support for micro effects of crowding.

Key Concepts

You should be able to explain the following concepts. You should also be prepared to cite several examples of each concept.

Urbanization 492	Fixed-rail metropolis 506
Preindustrial cities (characteristics) 494	Freeway metropolis 506
	Ethnic succession 511
Specialization 504	Index of dissimilarity 512
Suburb 505	_Gemeinschaft_ 514
Metropolitan area (metropolis) 505	_Gesellschaft_ 514
	Anomie 514
Sphere of influence 505	
Standard Metropolitan Statistical Area 505	

Key Research Studies

Be familiar with both the methodology and the results of the research studies cited here.

Darroch and Marston: test of theory of ethnic succession   511
Guest and Weed: economics and integration   511
Taeuber: test of Guest and Weed study   513
Macro studies of crowding   517
Gove and others: micro study of crowding   517

Key Theories

You should be able to explain the assumptions of these theories and, when applicable, cite related research findings.

Park and Burgess: theory of ethnic succession
Tonnies: _Gemeinschaft_ and _Gesellschaft_
Durkheim and Wirth: anomie theories

_____
Completion

1. The migration of people from the countryside to the city is termed _____.

2. _____ is the result of the more general process of _____.

3. The successive occupation of slum neighborhoods by the lowest status groups is termed _____.

4. Limits on the size of preindustrial cities included poor transportation and _____.

5. _____ and urbanization are inseparable processes.

6. An elaborate division of labor to simplify production is termed _____.

7. If an area has a population of more than 2,500, demographers classify it as a(n) _____.

8. The U.S. Census classifies a community as a city when it has at least _____ residents.

9. A city and its suburbs with their central city as a single unit is termed a(n) _____.

10. The _____ of a city is the area whose inhabitants depend on the central city for jobs, recreation, and a sense of community.

11. The focal point of the _____ metropolis was the center of the city.

12. Decentralized cities, common in the western United States, are termed _____.

13. The theory of ethnic succession was proposed by _____ and _____.

14. Park and Burgess suggested that ethnic and racial segregation in cities was based primarily on _____ and _____ differences.

15. Guest and Weed argued that _____ between groups seemed to be the primary barrier to neighborhood integration.

16. _____ and _____ argued that urban areas are characterized by high rates of anomie.

17. Gove and others found support for _____ rather than _____ theories of crowding.

18. Tonnies used the term _____ to describe small cohesive communities.

19. Tonnies used the term <u>Gesellschaft</u> to describe the quality of life in _____ societies.

20. An urban place in the immediate vicinity of a city is termed a(n) _____.

Multiple Choice

1. The size of preindustrial cities was limited by:
   a. disease
   b. poor transportation
   c. reliance on nearby farms to provide food
   d. a and b
   e. all of the above

2. Today approximately _____ of Americans and Canadians are urban residents.
   a. 25 percent
   b. 50 percent
   c. 60 percent
   d. 75 percent
   e. 90 percent

3. People were drawn to preindustrial cities because of:
   a. economic incentive
   b. the prospect of a more interesting and stimulating life
   c. the comparative safety of life in the city compared with the small town
   d. a and b
   e. all of the above

4. Industrialization:
   a. made it possible for most people to live in cities
   b. made it necessary for most people to live in cities
   c. depends upon specialization
   d. all of the above
   e. none of the above

5. According to the U.S. Census, a community must have at least _____ residents to qualify as a city.
   a. 2,500
   b. 20,000
   c. 50,000
   d. 75,000
   e. 100,000

6. If a locale has a population of more than 2,500, demographers
   term it a(n) _____.
   a. urban place
   b. urban area
   c. community
   d. city
   e. village

7. The area surrounding a city whose inhabitants depend on the
   central city for jobs, recreation, media, and a sense of
   community constitute the city's:
   a. metropolitan area
   b. sphere of influence
   c. metropolis
   d. zone of transition
   e. zone of influence

8. An area counts as a Standard Metropolitan Statistical Area if
   it:
   a. has a central city of 50,000 or more
   b. is surrounded by a county in which 75 percent of those
      working in the county work in agriculture
   c. is surrounded by a county in which 15 percent of the
      workers commute to the central city for work
   d. a and c
   e. all of the above

9. Fixed-rail cities:
   a. made the center of the city the focal point
   b. are common in the western United States
   c. are more evenly spread out than the freeway metropolis
   d. all of the above
   e. none of the above

10. According to the Gallup Poll, most Americans prefer to live:
    a. in a city
    b. on a farm
    c. in a suburb or small town
    d. b and c
    e. none of the above

11. The theory of ethnic succession is most closely associated
    with:
    a. Park and Burgess
    b. Tonnies
    c. Durkheim
    d. Wirth
    e. none of the above

12. The degree of segregation or integration of a neighborhood is measured by an:
    a. index of similarity
    b. index of dissimilarity
    c. index of status characteristics
    d. index of ethnic characteristics
    e. none of the above

13. Guest and Weed:
    a. argued that Park and Burgess were discussing individual upward mobility
    b. argued that the status inequality between groups seems to be the primary barrier to neighborhood integration
    c. found evidence that would discredit the theory of Park and Burgess
    d. a and b
    e. all of the above

14. Research on anomie in urban areas has found that:
    a. considerable support exists for anomie theories
    b. urbanites typically maintain close attachments to others
    c. anomie is characteristic of most urbanites
    d. a and c
    e. none of the above

15. Macro studies of crowding have found that:
    a. considerable support exists for the "psychic overload" theory
    b. city people are more prone to alcoholism and mental illness than are rural people
    c. neighborhoods with high population density have much higher rates of pathology than do less dense neighborhoods
    d. all of the above
    e. none of the above

16. The micro studies of Gove and others found that:
    a. there is little support for micro theories of crowding
    b. people in crowded homes have poorer mental health
    c. members of crowded homes have poorer social relations with each other
    d. b and c
    e. none of the above

17. The concepts of _Gemeinschaft_ and _Gesellschaft_ are associated with:
    a. Park and Burgess
    b. Tonnies
    c. Durkheim
    d. Wirth
    e. Guest and Weed

18. Which of the following is/are characteristic of <u>Gesellschaft</u>?
    a. People are united only by self-interest.
    b. Group members share little agreement about the norms and deviance is common.
    c. Human relationships are fleeting and manipulative.
    d. all of the above
    e. none of the above

19. Durkheim argued that:
    a. a primary consequence of urbanization was the breakdown of order
    b. urbanites live in a state of anomie
    c. rural areas have higher crime rates than urban areas
    d. a and b
    e. all of the above

20. Research by Gove and others on crowding found that:
    a. child care in crowded homes was poor
    b. the effects of crowding began to show up only when there were more than two people per room in a household
    c. people responded to crowding by withdrawing mentally and physically
    d. a and c
    e. all of the above

Essay

1. A. Define urbanization. (knowledge)
   B. Describe some characteristics of preindustrial cities. (comprehension)
   C. Discuss the interplay between urbanization and modernization. (analysis)

2. A. Name Park and Burgess's theory. (knowledge)
   B. Explain this theory. (comprehension)
   C. Show how recent research studies have (or have not) supported this theory. (analysis)

3. Discuss some characteristics of preindustrial cities and show how these characteristics limited their size.

4. Distinguish between Tonnies's concepts of <u>Gemeinschaft</u> and <u>Gesellschaft</u>.

5. Discuss macro and micro theories of crowding and cite relevant research findings.

Answers

Completion

1.	urbanization	11.	fixed-rail
2.	Urbanization, modernization	12.	freeway metropolises
3.	succession	13.	Park, Burgess
4.	disease	14.	economic, status
5.	Industrialization	15.	status inequality
6.	specialization	16.	Durkheim, Wirth
7.	urban place	17.	micro, macro
8.	50,000	18.	Gemeinschaft
9.	metropolis	19.	industrial
10.	sphere of influence	20.	suburb

Multiple Choice

1.	e	11.	a
2.	d	12.	b
3.	d	13.	b
4.	d	14.	b
5.	c	15.	e
6.	a	16.	d
7.	b	17.	b
8.	d	18.	d
9.	a	19.	d
10.	c	20.	d

CHAPTER 19
The Organizational Age

Overview

After describing the characteristics of formal organizations,
this chapter uses examples of the military, private business, and
government to describe the process of centralization in
nineteenth-century organizations. It then discusses Weber's
concept of rational bureaucracy and the rational systems
approach. This approach is contrasted with the natural systems
approach to the study of formal organizations. Chapter 19
considers next the process of decentralization in private
business and highlights the theories of Blau and Thompson. The
chapter closes with a look at the increasing centralization in
government.

Capsule Summary

Formal (or rational) organizations differ from older forms of
organization in that they apply reason to the problems of
management. Characteristics of formal organizations include the
following: a clear statement of goals, operating principles and
procedures for pursuing these goals, trained leaders, clear lines
of communication and authority, and written communication and
records. During the nineteenth century, formal organizations
emerged in such diverse areas as the military, private industry,
and the government.
     Max Weber termed these organizations rational bureaucracies.
His approach, often termed the rational system approach,
emphasizes the official and intended characteristics of an
organization. Social scientists have criticized the rational
approach as being too limited. People, they argue, do not behave
like machines. Rather, the general principles of the natural
behavior of people and groups apply to the behavior of
bureaucratic organizations. An important principle of this
natural system approach is that the rarely stated but overriding
goal of organizations is to survive. Adherents of the natural
approach focus on the processes of goal displacement, goal
conflict, and informal relations among members. Rather than
opposing one another, these two approaches are really
complementary views.
     Although the nineteenth century saw the centralization of
business and industry, more recently the trend in these
organizations has been one of decentralization. This process
relies on autonomous divisions, differentiation, and discretion.
The theories of Blau and Thompson, which have focused on this
process, have led to considerable empirical research.
     Ironically, while private businesses have become
increasingly decentralized, governments have tended to become

even more <u>centralized</u>. When applied to government, the terms <u>bureaucracy</u> and <u>bureaucrat</u> have a negative connotation in the minds of many people. Because governments are not as vulnerable as private organizations, recent critics have suggested that governments also should be subject to objective evaluations of performance.

Key Concepts

You should be able to explain the concepts listed here and be prepared to cite several examples of each concept.

Formal organization	521	Goal displacement	531
Rational organization	521	Goal conflict	532
Vertical integration	525	Span of control	536
Functional division	525	Diversified organization	537
Spoils system	528	Autonomous division	537
Bureaucracy	528	Decentralization	537
Rational system	530	Management by objectives	538
Natural system	531	Discretion	538

Key Theories

You should be prepared to explain the assumptions of these theories and, when applicable, cite related research findings.

Weber: rational system approach
Natural system approach
Blau: theory of organization
Thompson: decentralization, discretion, and coalition
          formation

Completion

1. The _____ organization applies reason to the problems of management.

2. During the _____ century the first large, formal organizations were created.

3. The political practice of giving public offices to _____ is termed the spoils system.

4. For Weber the term <u>bureaucracy</u> was inseparable from the term _____.

5. The rational system approach emphasizes the _____ and _____ characteristics of organizations.

6. The _____ system approach emphasizes the informal and unintended characteristics of organizations.

7. _____ occurs when organizations change their goals in pursuit of survival.

8. _____ occurs when different groups within an organization tend to pursue different goals.

9. The _____ system approach argues that the overriding goal of organizations is to survive.

10. The limit on the number of people a given person can supervise effectively is termed the _____.

11. The key element in the decentralization of organizations is _____.

12. Blau argued that the _____ the organization, the greater the proportion of total resources that must be devoted to management.

13. Discretion involves both the _____ for making decisions and the _____ to carry them out.

14. The more serious the potential consequences of an error are perceived to be, the _____ willing people will be to assume discretion.

15. Recently business has _____ while government has become increasingly _____.

16. The strength of private bureaucracies is their _____.

17. The organization of military troops into small, identical units, each containing all military elements, is an example of a(n) _____ system.

18. In an organization, _____ divisions each include a full set of functional divisions.

19. The dispersing of authority from a few central administrators to persons directly engaged in activities is termed _____.

20. A situation in which managers and subordinates agree on goals that subordinates will try to achieve is called _____.

1. During the _____ century, formal organizations
   developed in the military, business, and government.
   a. twentieth
   b. nineteenth
   c. eighteenth
   d. seventeenth
   e. sixteenth

2. Formal organizations differ from older forms of organization
   in that formal organizations:
   a. depend on a clear statement of goals
   b. possess clear lines of authority and communication
   c. use written records and communications
   d. a and c
   e. all of the above

3. Rational bureaucracy was first described by:
   a. Peter Blau
   b. Max Weber
   c. James Thompson
   d. Emile Durkheim
   e. none of the above

4. In the spoils system:
   a. the benefits of public office go to the supporters of
       winning politicians
   b. people are encouraged to make a career of government
       service
   c. people are prevented from making a career of government
       service
   d. a and b
   e. a and c

5. The _____ system approach emphasizes the informal and
   unintended characteristics of organizations.
   a. rational
   b. natural
   c. informal
   d. irrational
   e. unnatural

6. According to Weber, bureaucracy is based on:
   a. functional specialization
   b. a blurring of lines of authority
   c. managers promoted on the basis of the spoils system
   d. a and b
   e. all of the above

7. The rational approach has been criticized because:
    a. the real lines of communication in organizations are not always the same as those laid out on the organizational chart
    b. all members always pursue the same goals
    c. of the limited nature of this approach
    d. a and c
    e. all of the above

8. According to the natural system approach, the overriding goal of organizations is to:
    a. specialize
    b. self-destruct
    c. survive
    d. diversify
    e. a and d

9. The situation termed _____ may occur when different groups within an organization tend to pursue goals different from the goals of the organization.
    a. goal conflict
    b. goal displacement
    c. decentralization
    d. functional integration
    e. none of the above

10. A company that is _____ controls each step in the process of bringing its products to the consumer.
    a. horizontally integrated
    b. decentralized
    c. vertically integrated
    d. functionally disintegrated
    e. none of the above

11. When the March of Dimes changed its focus from the elimination of polio to the elimination of birth defects, it exhibited:
    a. functional integration
    b. goal displacement
    c. goal conflict
    d. horizontal integration
    e. rationalization

12. A major shortcoming of the rational system approach is that it fails to emphasize:
    a. the formal structure
    b. goal displacement
    c. the organizational blueprint
    d. b and c
    e. all of the above

13. The limit of the number of people that a given person can supervise effectively is termed the:
   a. functional limit
   b. span of control
   c. vertical integration limit
   d. supervisory sphere
   e. none of the above

14. In order to survive, the DuPont company had to institute:
   a. centralization
   b. functional limits
   c. autonomous divisions
   d. supervisory spheres
   e. all of the above

15. In his theory of administrative growth, Blau argued that:
   a. as organizations become more diversified, the size of administrative components increases relative to the size of other components
   b. the smaller the organization, the greater the proportion of total resources that must be devoted to management function
   c. organizational growth causes differentiation
   d. a and c
   e. all of the above

16. Thompson argued that members of an organization will accept discretion when:
   a. they believe they cannot adequately control conditions affecting decisions
   b. they do not share the responsibility of that decision with others
   c. the decision involves forces outside the organization
   d. a and c
   e. all of the above

17. Which of the following statements is/are true?
   a. As governmental organizations have grown larger, they have decentralized.
   b. Centralization has dominated governmental organizations while decentralization has dominated private organizations.
   c. As governmental organizations have grown larger, they have become more centralized.
   d. b and c
   e. none of the above

18. Breaking an organization into smaller units on the basis of specialized activities is termed:
   a. decentralization
   b. natural system approach
   c. geographical division
   d. functional divisions
   e. none of the above

19. When the official goals of an organization are ignored or changed, it is termed:
    a. goal conflict
    b. goal rejection
    c. goal replacement
    d. goal displacement
    e. none of the above

20. The rational system approach emphasizes:
    a. the intended characteristics of the organization
    b. the informal characteristics of the organization
    c. the unintended characteristics of the organization
    d. a and b
    e. b and c

Essay

1. A. Name the two approaches to the study of bureaucracy. (knowledge)
   B. Explain each of these approaches. (comprehension)
   C. Contrast these approaches. (analysis)

2. A. Define formal organization. (knowledge)
   B. Describe four official and intended characteristics of formal organizations. (comprehension)
   C. Apply these characteristics to the military, government, and/or private industry. (application)

3. Describe the characteristics of formal organizations that distinguish them from older forms of organization.

4. Using the examples in the text, trace the development of formal organization in the military, private business, and government.

5. Explain the process of decentralization. Discuss either the theory of Blau or Thompson on the decentralization process.

Answers

Completion

1. formal or rational
2. nineteenth
3. supporters of the winning politician
4. rationality
5. official, intended
6. natural
7. Goal displacement
8. Goal conflict
9. natural
10. span of control
11. discretion
12. larger
13. responsibility, authority
14. less
15. decentralized, centralized
16. vulnerability
17. divisional
18. autonomous
19. decentralization
20. management by objectives

Multiple Choice

1. b
2. e
3. d
4. e
5. b
6. a
7. d
8. c
9. a
10. c
11. b
12. b
13. b
14. c
15. d
16. b
17. d
18. d
19. d
20. a

CHAPTER 20
Collective Behavior and Social Movements

Overview
_____

This chapter, written by William Sims Bainbridge, offers a
conceptual framework for analyzing collective behavior and social
movements. It starts with a description of this framework and
distinguishes among parallel behavior, collective behavior, and
social movements. It describes the various forms of collective
behavior--panics, crazes, and riots--and offers in-depth accounts
of historical examples of each. Chapter 20 then discusses the
rise of Nazism as an example of a successful mass movement. It
concludes with a description of the rise of a successful elite
movement, the spaceflight movement, in which Bainbridge presents
material drawn from his research and lifelong interest in
rocketry and spaceflight.

Capsule Summary
_____

Often groups of people engage in unusual behavior in an attempt
to encourage, prevent, or react to social change. When this
behavior occurs spontaneously, with little or no organization or
planning, it is termed collective behavior. When it is of longer
duration, planned, and organized, it is termed a social movement.
Parallel behavior, on the other hand, lacks the element of group
interaction, which characterizes both collective behavior and
social movements. Through increased focused interaction,
parallel behavior may be transformed into collective behavior, a
social movement, and ultimately a social institution. In
reality, however, few collective actions succeed in this fashion.
     Collective behavior includes crazes (or fads), panics, and
riots. Crazes occur when a number of people rush toward
something they desire. Frisbees, Hula Hoops, and tulips have all
been the focus of crazes. Panics, on the other hand, occur when
people flee from real or imagined danger. Often, as in the case
of the "War of the Worlds" broadcast or the Barseback nuclear
incident, reactions to panics are overestimated. Riots occur
when a crowd threatens or attacks persons or property. The Nika
uprising and the case of the Luddites are examples of riots.
     The Nazi movement is an example of a successful mass
movement. To grow, mass movements rely on a natural constituency
from which to draw members and an internal society capable of
attracting and incorporating new members. Social conditions and
the political structure of Germany after World War I provided the
Nazis with both. Drawing on its strength in the middle class,
Nazism grew from an obscure movement among many other movements
to a mass movement that temporarily controlled and dominated an
entire society.

Not all successful social movements are mass movements drawing their support from oppressed groups or a discontented middle class. Some, like the spaceflight movement, are elite movements, which draw their support from the dominant social and political structures. Bainbridge's study of this movement drew upon previously published accounts of the history of rocketry and his own lifelong interest in the subject. Through his research, he was able to show how this movement developed around an opportunity and grew into a successful movement. By showing how highly dedicated and gifted people can use opportunities to further their own interests, his research has called into question some of the assumptions of technological determinism.

Key Concepts

Be prepared to explain the following concepts and be able to cite several examples of each concept.

Riot 544		National constituency	561
Social movement 548		Internal society 561	
Collective behavior	548	Interactive model 570	
Parallel behavior	549	First-generation leader	572
Craze 550		Second-generation leader	572
Panic 552		Ideologue 572	
Crowd behavior	552	Executive 572	
Summary event	553	Technological determinism	573
Ideology 560			

Key Examples

Rather than discussing specific theories or contributions, this chapter offers a conceptual framework for understanding collective behavior and social movements. You should be thoroughly familiar with this framework and be able to apply it to specific situations. You should also be able to identify these examples, explain the course of events that occurred, and show how they illustrate the various characteristics of collective behavior and social movements.

Flagpole sitting   547
Tulipomania   550
"War of the Worlds"   552
Barseback nuclear incident   554
Nika uprising   556
Luddites   558
Nazi movement   560
Spaceflight movement   568

1. Flagpole sitting is an example of a phenomenon termed a(n) _____ or _____.

2. Behavior that tends to be brief, episodic, and unorganized is termed _____.

3. Organized groups dedicated to _____ or _____ social change are called social movements.

4. Situations in which terrified people attempt to flee danger are known as _____.

5. In a(n) _____, people rush toward something they all desire.

6. A hostile outburst of collective behavior in which a crowd of people threatens or attacks other persons or property is termed a(n) _____.

7. Collective behavior tends to be brief, _____, and _____.

8. _____ are sustained by organization and planning; they often endure for a long time.

9. _____ occurs when each person is doing the same thing for the same reason but each is doing it alone.

10. The "War of the Worlds" broadcast and the Barseback nuclear incident are examples of _____.

11. Panic is most likely when an ambiguous threat is seen as _____.

12. A concrete representation of a vague but intense social and emotional situation is called a(n) _____.

13. A segment of the population that lacks effective representation is termed a(n) _____ for a mass movement.

14. Systems of beliefs and values that passively influence a social movement are termed _____.

15. A cohesive network of social relationships within a movement is called a(n) _____.

16. Conditions necessary for the growth of a mass movement include _____ and a natural constituency.

17. Social disorganization on a large scale often leads to _____ on a small scale.

18. The type of leader who functions to build and guide a social enterprise is termed a(n) _____.

19. The spaceflight movement drew its interest and support primarily from the _____ classes.

20. _____ is the belief that technological change is automatic and that when the time is right for the next step forward it will occur.

Multiple Choice

1. Actions may be related to social change when:
   a. the action may be aimed at preventing social change
   b. the action may be undertaken to cause social change
   c. the action itself may be a social change
   d. a and b
   e. all of the above

2. Primary reasons for doing sociology include:
   a. understanding the interplay between the individual and society
   b. proving that we are entirely creations of our society and that our history determines our destiny
   c. making social life less mysterious
   d. a and c
   e. all of the above

3. In order for a behavior to be classified as collective behavior:
   a. the individuals must have no influence over each other
   b. there must be little or no planning
   c. the action may be taken by lone individuals as well as groups
   d. a and c
   e. all of the above

4. Collective behavior and social movements differ:
   a. in the degree of planning
   b. in their length and duration
   c. in their degree of organization
   d. a and c
   e. all of the above

5. When people are doing the same thing for the same reason but each person is doing it alone, it is referred to as:
   a. collective behavior
   b. parallel behavior
   c. a social movement
   d. a reactionary movement
   e. isolated behavior

6. In a _____, a group of people rush toward something
    they desire.
    a. panic
    b. craze
    c. riot
    d. parallel behavior
    e. none of the above

7. In a _____, people rush away from something they fear.
    a. panic
    b. craze
    c. riot
    d. parallel behavior
    e. none of the above

8. The cases of the Luddites and the Nika uprising are examples
    of:
    a. crazes
    b. riots
    c. panics
    d. parallel behavior
    e. none of the above

9. A concrete representation of a vague but intense social and
    emotional situation is termed a(n):
    a. natural constituency
    b. internal society
    c. summary event
    d. precipitating incident
    e. precipitating event

10. In a social movement, a cohesive network of social
    relationships capable of attracting and incorporating
    large numbers of new members is termed a(n):
    a. natural constituency
    b. internal society
    c. collective coalition
    d. ideological supporter
    e. none of the above

11. Conditions that are necessary for the growth of a mass
    movement include:
    a. a strong ideology to recruit new members
    b. a vigorous internal society
    c. natural constituency
    d. b and c
    e. all of the above

12. The spaceflight movement:
    a. began as parallel behavior
    b. was created by oppressed groups
    c. had a strong natural constituency from which to draw
       support
    d. all of the above
    e. none of the above

13. Successful social movements:
    a. are always mass movements
    b. are always created by oppressed groups
    c. always draw their strength from the misery of some
       natural constituency
    d. all of the above
    e. none of the above

14. Which of the following statements is/are not true?
    a. Social movements are always drawn from oppressed people.
    b. Ideology plays a very active role in the formation of
       most social movements.
    c. Almost all social movements are successful.
    d. all of the above
    e. none of the above

15. Smelser termed the type of leader who invents and spreads
    ideas the _____ leader.
    a. ideologue
    b. executive
    c. expressive
    d. instrumental
    e. none of the above

16. Technological determinists claim that:
    a. changes in technology are the cause of all social change
    b. technological change is self-generating
    c. unusually talented people often speed up the pace of
       innovation
    d. a and b
    e. all of the above

17. The Nazi movement's greatest strength was in the _____
    class.
    a. lower
    b. working
    c. middle
    d. upper
    e. <u>Lumpenproletariat</u>

18. Bainbridge gathered most of his data on the spaceflight
    movement from:
    a. interviews
    b. participant observation
    c. books
    d. visits to rocket installations
    e. none of the above

19. Which of the following is a typical sequence of events in a successful social movement?
    a. parallel behavior, collective behavior, social movement, social institution
    b. social movement, collective behavior, parallel behavior
    c. social movement, collective behavior, social institution
    d. parallel behavior, social institution, social movement
    e. parallel behavior, collective behavior, social institution, social movement

20. The rise of Nazism was fostered by:
    a. a strong ideology that helped recruit new members at the beginning of the movement
    b. a political system that encouraged the development of many political parties
    c. its appeal to the lower class
    d. a and b
    e. all of the above

Essay

1. A. Explain the interactive model. (comprehension)
    B. Apply the interactive model to the spaceflight movement. (application)
    C. Compare and contrast the spaceflight movement with the Nazi movement. (analysis)

2. A. Name three types of collective behavior. (knowledge)
    B. Give examples of these three types. (comprehension)
    C. Compare and contrast collective behavior and social movement. (analysis)

3. Discuss the criteria that must be met for a behavior to be considered collective behavior.

4. Using an example (real or fictitious), trace the sequence of events that occur as parallel behavior is transformed into a social institution.

5. Using the material presented in this chapter, respond to the following question: "Do we make our history or does it make us?"

Answers

Completion

1.	craze, fad	11.	immediate
2.	collective behavior	12.	summary event
3.	causing, preventing	13.	natural constituency
4.	panics	14.	ideologies
5.	craze	15.	internal society
6.	riot	16.	internal society
7.	episodic, unorganized	17.	increased social organization
8.	Social movements	18.	executive
9.	Parallel behavior	19.	middle and upper
10.	panics	20.	Technological determinism

Multiple Choice

1.	e	11.	d
2.	d	12.	a
3.	b	13.	e
4.	e	14.	d
5.	b	15.	a
6.	b	16.	d
7.	a	17.	c
8.	b	18.	c
9.	c	19.	a
10.	b	20.	b

CHAPTERS 16 TO 20
Review and Special Project

Review
___

This section focused on changes brought about by modernization.
It described population trends, urban growth and development, the
centralization and decentralization of organizations, and
collective behavior and social movements.

Special Project
___

Rapid shifts in population can cause changes in society. Special
Topic 6 focused upon many of the changes brought about by the
"baby boom." During the 1960s, colleges and universities
experienced growth and change as the baby boom generation entered
college. During the 1970s and early 1980s, many colleges
experienced declining enrollment among traditional college
students. This decline necessitated further change.
    You might wish to study the impact that this group and its
passing had on some aspects of your college or university.
Possible areas to investigate include the following suggestions.

1. Demographic changes in the composition of students and
    faculty (age, race, sex, marital status, and so on).
2. Building expansion or changes in the use of physical
    space.
3. Curriculum changes and changes in degree requirements.
4. The increase (or decrease) of different categories of
    students in specific majors or programs.
5. Increased (or decreased) interest and participation in
    social movements and political activism.
6. Increased (or decreased) interest and participation in
    student organizations such as sororities and
    fraternities.
7. Changes in the organizational structure of some
    components of the school.

Possible sources of information and data for the topic you choose
could include: student profiles and demographic data available
from administrative offices, interviews with faculty,
administrators, former and current students, college catalogues,
maps, curriculum information, sorority and fraternity records,
and college newspapers. Of course, the changes you will observe
are the result of the complex interaction of societal changes
that have occurred over the past two decades. You will want to
incorporate these changes into your explanation of changes on
your campus.

A Message to Our Users

Professor William Sims Bainbridge and Wadsworth Publishing Company have joined in a commitment to publish this high-quality software at an affordable price. Because copy protection would have increased the price, we have not protected the disk. We are thus trusting you to observe the copyright laws by making copies only for your own use on one computer at a time.

Please help us continue to produce quality software by sending us your responses to the software and ideas for expanding or improving it or new ways to use it. Thanks for working with us.

Stu Thomas
Software Development Manager
Wadsworth Publishing Company
10 Davis Drive
Belmont, CA 94002

Experiments in Sociology:
Five Computer Simulations

William Sims Bainbridge
Harvard University

Contents

Sociology students have long been a deprived and disadvantaged group. Physics and chemistry courses offer weekly laboratory hours in which students do experiments with the materials and principles explained in their textbooks—playing with spectacular electricity and smelly chemicals—gaining real life experience of their subjects rather than merely reading about them. But sociology students have had no laboratories.

Now, through the technology of microcomputers, we can simulate actual sociological research, even create "toy societies" of imaginary humans to experiment upon. Professor Stark's introductory sociology textbook explains how social scientists actually do their research, develop their theories, and make their discoveries. This set of microcomputer simulations, designed to accompany Stark's text, will let you experience some of the excitement, mystery, and accomplishment of real sociological research.

One is a questionnaire study of juvenile delinquency, two are demographic simulations of population growth, one is a survey to explore the differences between your attitudes and those of your friends, and one examines the spread of social movements through a community. But each of them draws upon several parts of the textbook, and we will refer to specific textbook pages in brackets. For example, "[245]" refers to page 245, about toy societies.

If you are not familiar with computers, do not panic. One of the joys of personal computers is that you can learn in private, exploring the possibilities in a mood of fun without feeling that more knowledgeable students may be laughing at your first halting steps. Sometimes, if you make a mistake the computer can recognize, it will beep at you. But this is just to alert you to try again and is not to be taken as an insult. The machine is your partner in research and your tool. Read the instructions carefully, especially those that appear on the computer's screen.

The worst that can happen, when you make a mistake, is that you'll have to start that part of your work over again. And I have anticipated many of the problems you might have in order to prevent them. Clear instructions will appear on the computer screen, and this study guide contains full instructions to take you every step of the way. The simulations are designed for beginning students, but they all have options of special interest to advanced students and instructors. Therefore, you don't have to learn all the alternatives, only the ones required for the modest assigned research projects.

I have called these research simulations *Experiments in Sociology* to emphasize that you can experiment with them, comparing the results of many different alternatives you might try. Of course, there is a particular research approach technically known as the experimental method [75–77], and some of your studies will use very different approaches. As a test of your understanding of different kinds of research, you might want to decide whether a particular project you do is really an "experiment" in this technical sense of the term. But you can adopt an experimental, exploratory mood with all of these programs, exercising your imagination as well as demonstrating your comprehension of the sociological principles.

Welcome to our research team! Good sociological experimenting!

Getting Started

You will need the right kind of computer, but I have written the programs to work on both of the types commonly found at colleges, the IBM and the Apple IIe/IIc/IIGS. One side of your disk will work with the Apple IIe, IIc, and IIGS (with 80-column text). The other side will work with the IBM and true IBM compatibles, if you have 128K of memory and DOS 2.1 or later. A graphics card is not required for the IBM, but if you have a color IBM monitor you will see the displays in colors.

There are a number of differences between the Apple II format and the IBM format, but the programs were designed to work nearly the same (and equally well) on both. For example, there is an important key on the computer's keyboard that tells the machine to go ahead and do the next thing on its list of tasks. It is found to the right of the ordinary letter keys and is usually bigger than any of them. On Apples, this is called the "Return key" and typically has the word RETURN written on it. IBMs have the same key, but it is called the "Enter" key. On many IBMs, it is marked with a hooked arrow pointing to the left. This can be confusing, because many of these IBMs have another arrow key right above it, the backspace key. We will call this the RETURN/ENTER key. Find the RETURN/ENTER key on your machine. It is the only special computer key you need to use. The other keys you will press are the familiar letter and num- ber keys of the ordinary typewriter.

The procedure for starting *Experiments in Sociology* is different on Apples and IBMs, so you should follow the instructions for your particular type of machine. With either type, find the main disk drive, sometimes labeled Drive I or Drive A (on Apple IIc's, the only drive built into the computer).

The following paragraphs tell you how to start up on each brand of machine, and how to make a per- sonal back-up copy of the disk in case an accident ruins the original disk. NOTE: Wadsworth Publishing Company has taken out a copyright on the programs as well as on this book, and it is illegal to make copies to give or sell to other people. Also, if you operate a microcomputer facility with many machines, you do *not* have the legal right to make copies (by any means, not just by producing disks containing the programs) so that different people may use the programs simultaneously.

We have produced this software at low cost so that it will be no burden for you to buy it, and we have made it possible for you to make a back-up copy for your convenience. Please do not take advantage of us. You would be breaking the law and risking serious consequences, just as you would in any other kind of theft. We think you will find the small cost of *Experiments in Sociology* well worth while.

Apple Computers_____

On Apples, put the *Experiments in Sociology* disk into the disk drive. If you have a machine with a switch for 40-column or 80-column text display, start it out with 40-column. Then simply turn the machine on. If it is already on, press the appropriate keys to "boot" the disk, as explained in your Apple instruction manuals.

To copy the disk, simply use the COPYA program on the DOS 3.3 disk that may have come with your machine, or a similar, standard program for copying disks.

IBM and IBM-Compatible Computers_____

With IBMs, you first have to load DOS (the Disk Operating System) into the computer. One way is to place the DOS disk, that came with the machine, into Drive A, then start it up. After a pause and various activity on the computer screen, you may be asked for the date and time. To respond to these questions, just press RETURN/ENTER. Eventually, "A>_" should appear on the IBM screen, meaning the machine is ready to do something with Drive A. Remove the DOS disk from Drive A, and insert the *Experiments in Sociology* disk. Now type GO and press RETURN/ENTER.

Here's how to make a back-up copy, with the disk operating system on it for your convenience. If you don't plan to do this, skip down to the next section in these instructions. But a back-up, "self-booting" copy will be easy to use. When you have made one, you can run the programs by simply placing the disk in Drive A and switching on the machine.

The following instructions explain how to make such a copy on a computer system with two double-sided disk drives. If you have a single drive system, or if you want to copy everything onto a hard disk or 3.5 inch microdisk, consult your DOS and computer system manuals. If you have an IBM compatible, you may have to consult them as well.

(1) Start the IBM-type machine with the DOS disk in the main disk drive (Drive A). After the whirring stops and you have hit the RETURN/ENTER key in response to questions about the time and date, you will see "A>_" on the screen.

(2) Type "FORMAT B:/S" and then press the RETURN/ENTER key. The disk will whir and you will be prompted to insert a blank disk in the second drive (Drive B) and hit any key to proceed. You will need a double-sided disk, to hold all the programs plus DOS. Make sure you insert a blank disk because everything on it will be erased. Then press any key, and the computer will go to work. Shortly, you will be asked if you want to format another disk. Respond with "N" for No, and you will again see "A>_" on the screen.

(3) Now replace the DOS disk in Drive A with your *Experiments in Sociology* disk. After doing this, type "COPY *.* B:" and hit RETURN/ENTER. Note that the spaces are important—one after the Y and one before the B. Both drives will go into action now. When this is done, "A>_" will appear on the screen again. The disk in Drive B is now your "autostarting working copy" of *Experiments in Sociology*.

Ready to Run the Disk

So, now you have placed a program disk in the main disk drive, whether an original or a copy, and have told the computer to start it up. The disk drive will whir, and in a moment the Wadsworth Publishing Company symbol will appear on the screen, followed a moment later by a title page, a copyright notice page, then what we call the MAIN MENU. This is a list of the five programs of the disk, headed by the question "Which experiment do you want?" There are five choices, numbered 1 through 5.

Notice that the number in front of each of the five choices is surrounded by a box. On most machines, you see a dark number in a bright box. This is my way of telling you which keys you can press, and you will see boxes around letter keys and RETURN/ENTER in the programs telling you that you may press the keys they represent. Each boxed number represents a key. Thus, you can press either the 1, 2, 3, 4, or 5 key. Just to see what happens, try typing some other number like a 6. The computer will beep, complaining about your error, then give you a chance to try again. Now press the key you really want and start one of the following simulations.

If you start the wrong simulation, because you pressed the wrong key, it is easy to switch to the one you really want. Of course, you could start over from the very beginning, but there is a quicker solution. You can switch immediately, by pressing a single key. The fourth simulation, a survey of you and your friends, starts with a menu of choices (made by pressing one of the number keys), including "switch to a different experiment." The other simulations have a hidden feature at the very beginning. You can escape these simulations and select the right one, by pressing the ESCAPE key, a special key often labeled ESCAPE or ESC, usually near the top-left corner of the keyboard. This works only at the very beginning of a simulation.

Two or three research exercise projects are suggested for each of the simulations, and five report forms are provided at the end of these instructions for your results. When doing a project for your class, you should prepare a two-page description of how you did the project, including any discoveries or sociological insights it stimulated. These can be the basis for lively class discussions or passed in with the report form as a written assignment. The programs are designed so you can invent many other projects.

1.   JUVENILE DELINQUENCY QUESTIONNAIRE_____

This simulation shows how sociological questionnaires are analyzed. One of the best and most influential questionnaire studies of recent years was designed by criminologist Travis Hirschi to examine the causes of juvenile delinquency [89]. Hirschi carefully wrote a large questionnaire, administered it to over two thousand high school boys, and collected other data on the respondents from their school and the police. Hirschi's study, *Causes of Delinquency*, tested three competing theories of deviant behavior that play very important roles in Stark's text: control theory [179], strain theory [178], and cultural (or subcultural) deviance theory [176].

We have a simplified version of Hirschi's questionnaire, twenty questions long, and two different simulated high schools we can administer it to, one in Virginia and the other in Washington state. One reason for using simulated data is to offer strong, clear results from a modest analysis, and you should not worry about whether real high schools are as delinquent as ours. Because the two schools are in very different social environments, the results will come out distinctly differently, illustrating, for example, Stark's discussion of regional differences in the power of religion [91].

The disk contains simulated data on 300 boys from each of the schools, but we will work with a random sample of just 100 boys. Sociologists seldom have the resources to ask their questions of everybody, and they have found that a random sample is almost as good [89]. The program can produce 2,000 different samples for each high school (different combinations of 100 boys out of the 300), and the results will be realistically slightly different for each sample. However, if the student and instructor wish, they may easily draw the same sample again, to extend or check their work.

NOTE: Your disk contains data very different from those published in the first edition of *Experiments in Sociology*, so results will come out very differently than if you were using the old edition. Also, the IBM data and Apple data differ slightly. The general shape of the results will be the same, but the samples of boys you get with different random numbers are *not* the same on an Apple as on an IBM machine.

A Trial Run _____

Start the disk and select "Juvenile delinquency questionnaire." After the computer has read the right program off the disk, a question will appear: "Which high school do you want to study?" Press the "1" key to select the Virginia school. Now the computer asks for a 4-digit number, such as the last four digits of a phone number. I suggest you type the last four digits of your telephone number. Different 4-digit numbers will select different samples of boys.

The disk drive will whir for a while, as we administer the questionnaire to the sample of 100 boys. Then the computer will go through the equivalent of punching the data onto cards or computer tape. In real research, this is tough work, so don't feel impatient.

Before too long, the screen will fill with questions. On Apples, you get the first 10 questions immediately, and you have to press RETURN to get the other 10. On IBMs you get all 20 questions right away. Each one can be answered "Yes" or "No," and you can see how many of the 100 boys gave each response. Because there are 100 boys, the number who said "Yes" is exactly the same as the percent who did.

Notice question #10, "Attends church often." I just started the program on my IBM, surveying the Virginia school, and typed in a random number. Of the 100 boys sampled, 59 said "Yes, I attend church often," while the other 41 said, "No, I don't attend church often."

Number 11 is also about religion. (Remember, on Apples you have to press RETURN for questions 11–20.) Fifty-seven of the boys believe "God punishes our sins," while 43 do not believe this. These two questions will be the focus of our trial run. When you are ready, press RETURN/ ENTER to get rid of the questions and go on to our basic analysis table.

We are going to analyze the twenty questions two at a time, to see if there is a connection between them—what we call a correlation. Do boys who say "yes" to question X also say "yes" to question Y? If they tend to do so, there is a correlation between X and Y [77–78]. We can test theories by checking if such a correlation exists. Does poverty cause delinquency? We can test this theory by seeing if boys who say they are poor also tend to be delinquent.

Each time, you will select one question to be the "X variable" (such as being poor) and another question to be the "Y variable" (being delinquent). For students who want to think technically, the X variable will be the cause or independent variable, and the Y variable will be the effect or dependent variable [76]. At the top of the screen, a message tells you to select these two variables, and at the bottom are instructions about typing in the number of the question that will be variable X. Suppose you don't remember what the questions are? On IBMs, they will be listed along the left side of the screen. On Apples, simply press the "Q" key to get a list of the questions.

Let's pick question #10 to be X and #11 to be Y. To do so, first type "10" and press RETURN/ ENTER. Now type "11" followed by RETURN/ENTER. The computer calculates for an instant, then displays the basic table with the results of your first analysis.

Look in the four boxes (what sociologists technically call the "cells" of the table). How many boys go to church often? Those listed in the YES column under the question "Attends church often." And how many do not? Those listed in the NO column. And how many believe God punishes our sins? Those in the YES row, to the right of "Believes God punishes our sins." And how many don't believe? Those in the NO row.

Consider the following hypothesis: Going to church makes boys believe God punishes our sins. Are the results in the table in line with this hypothesis, or do they falsify it [63]? Certainly, we see a lot of boys who go to church often and do believe, and a lot of boys who neither attend church nor believe. There are not very many boys who go to church but don't believe, and few who believe but do not go to church. There seems to be an association.

One way to see the results more clearly is to compare the percentage of believers among those who go to church often with the percentage among those who do not attend often. You could calculate these easily by hand, but the computer is happy to do that job for you. Press the "P" key and the percents will appear. Among church-goers, a high percentage probably believe God punishes our sins, but only a small percentage of those who do not attend church often have this belief.

Another way to look at the results is through correlations, a method explained [73–74, 77–78] and used [187] in Professor Stark's book. I have provided basic introductions to correlations in both of my recent software publications, *Experiments in Psychology* and *Sociology Laboratory*. Either of those might be useful for beginning sociology students. But a very quick introduction might be useful here.

Suppose you were studying the physical characteristics of the 100 high school boys in your sample. You measured each one and wrote down his height and weight. You might guess that height and weight are related; tall boys tend to be heavier than short boys. But you know that this is not a perfect association. You can't guess somebody's weight very exactly merely from seeing how tall he is. Some tall boys are lighter than some short boys, because some tall boys are skinny, while some short ones are fat. Height is associated with weight, but how strongly?

A correlation coefficient is a simple little number that expresses the strength and direction of the relationship between two variables. For example, the correlation between height and weight in your sample of 100 boys might be 0.50. A positive number (greater than zero) like this would tell you that tall boys tend to be heavier—that height and weight tend to go together, in the same direction. Height is a variable, because different boys may have different heights, and weight is another variable. As height increases, going from boy to boy, weight tends to increase as well. As height decreases, weight tends to decrease.

If tall boys were always heavier than short boys, and you could easily predict a boy's weight from his height, then the correlation would perhaps be 1.00. If there were no relationship between height and weight, then the correlation could be dead zero, or very close to it.

It is also possible to get negative correlations, numbers between 0.00 and –1.00. Suppose you had a sample of 100 adult men, of various ages. Chances are that the older men would have less hair than the younger men. Suppose you studied each of these guys, writing down his age and the number of hairs on his head. You might find a correlation of –0.50 between years of age and hairs on the head. The more years a man has in him, the fewer hairs he will tend to have on his head. Here, the variables are age and hairiness, and they have a negative correlation.

With the computer program simulating a delinquency study, you will become familiar with correlations by using them. To get the correlation between your two questionnaire variables, press the "C" key. I just did this, and a little message appeared near the left edge of the screen: "r = 0.67." This means that there is a positive correlation of .67 between going to church and believing God punishes sins, for my sample of 100 high school boys. The "r" means that this coefficient is Pearson's r, perhaps the most commonly used correlation coefficient.

After "r = 0.67" I see "Significance: 1 in 1000." This means the correlation is "statistically significant" [78]. There is only 1 chance in 1000 that bad luck gave us a false impression of a correlation. In general, we can have great confidence in correlations that are this highly significant. Sometimes you will get "Significance: 1 in 100." This is pretty solid, too. At other times the odds against our result being bad are lower: "Significance: 1 in 20" or "Significance: 1 in 10." Don't have much confidence in such cases. When you see "Not significant," you know the coefficient is not significantly different from zero.

Pearson's r is not the only correlation coefficient. There are several others each with its own technical advantages and disadvantages. Advanced students and instructors might like to see what one of the others looks like for this table, so I have included gamma. Notice that the instructions at the bottom of the screen say "Press... C for Correlations." Press the "C" and gamma will replace r in the upper left. Pressing "C" again will take gamma away and leave the area blank. Press "C" a third time to get r back.

Most students will want to stick with Pearson's r, and you should not worry about the fact that r and gamma will be different numbers. Advanced students please note that the test of statistical significance for gamma is actually chi square, and it is generally considered bad form to calculate chi square for tables that have one or more nearly empty cells (fewer than 5 cases). Therefore, gamma will appear without a message about significance for some extreme tables.

To complete this trial run, you might want to produce a few more tables reporting on other variables. To get rid of the results you already got, simply press RETURN/ENTER. Now you're back in position to select new X and Y variables (on Apples, you might press "Q" to see the full list of questions again). Finally, when screen instructions permit, you can press the "S" key (for stop) to end the trial run.

The Logic of Hirschi's Research

Travis Hirschi says the study of deviant behavior has traditionally been oriented toward three types of sociological theory—and Stark discusses these at length. According to control or bond theories, a person is free to commit delinquent acts because his ties to the conventional order have somehow been broken [179]. According to cultural deviance theories, the deviant individual conforms to a set of standards not accepted by a larger or more powerful society [176]. According to *strain* or motivational theories, legitimate desires that conformity cannot satisfy force a person into deviance [178].

Many of Hirschi's questions were designed to measure concepts in one or another of these three theories. But first, he had to measure delinquency. One way he did so was to ask each boy a number of questions about particular acts he might have performed. Has he stolen something? Has he driven somebody's car without permission? Has he vandalized property? Has he beaten somebody up? Many of the boys said they had not done any of these, while some had done quite a few. The fourth simulation in this set lets you see how he combined questions about all of these into a single "self-report" measure of delinquency. But you can't always trust what people say, so Hirschi also got information from the police about which boys had ever been picked up.

Thus, our simplified study has two questions about delinquency. The first of these asked the boy himself to report about any delinquent acts he had done, while the second is based on official police records:

     1. Self-reported delinquent?

     2. Picked up by police?

The key idea of control theory is that boys who are strongly attached to other people [79, 180] and committed to conventional institutions like school will be prevented from engaging in delinquent acts by these bonds. Five of our questions are relevant here:

     4. Likes school?

     7. Mother supervises closely?

     8. Intimate communication with father?

     16. Low aptitude test scores?

     19. Drinks alcohol?

A boy is strongly attached to a parent if his mother supervises him closely or if he enjoys much intimate communication with his father. These personal bonds will inhibit delinquency, according to control theory. If the boy likes school, then he is attached to his teachers and has invested a good deal of effort in doing well, an investment he would stand to lose if he became delinquent. But boys with low aptitude test scores at school may do poorly in classes, be rejected by teachers, and stand to lose very little if they violate the law. A boy who drinks alcohol at this age (at least in many communities) has clearly broken with the restrictions of childhood and does not submit to the controlling force of norms adults want children to follow.

Cultural deviance theory assumes that there exists a delinquent subculture of boys who influence each other to commit delinquent acts. Seven of our questions bear on this theory, some more directly than others.

     3. Thinks of self as delinquent?

     9. Wants to be like his friends?

     12. Teachers like his friends?

     14. Police have picked up his friends?

     15. Thinks breaking the law is okay?

     17. Respects best friends' opinions?

     18. Believes in living for today?

A member of a delinquent subculture thinks that breaking the law is okay, because lawbreaking is part of his culture. Commitment to a future conventional career that requires self-denial for years is not part of the delinquent culture, whose members believe in living for today. These opinions should be reinforced by delinquent friends, who are an important reference group [56], so we would expect that a delinquent's friends have often been picked up by the police and that teachers do not like his friends. Some versions of cultural deviance theory argue that the delinquent is really playing a standard role in his subculture—that of delinquent boy—and thus that he should think of himself as a delinquent.

189

Mere evidence that delinquents have delinquent friends does not prove that the boys' delinquency was caused by association with these friends. Perhaps, as the old saying goes, birds of a feather flock together. That is, boys who are already delinquent come together, perhaps not trusting each other very much, because they are rejected by the "good kids." Therefore, if cultural deviance theory is true, we should expect that delinquent boys are just as likely as nondelinquents to respect their best friends' opinions and to want to be like their friends.

Strain theory says that all boys want to achieve success, to fulfill the American dream of a good education and the high income it can bring, but that boys from the lower classes find it especially difficult to succeed. The result is great frustration which may express itself in vandalism or other delinquency. Also, if poor kids decide they never can gain wealth by legitimate means (getting a good education and working hard), they may turn to the illegitimate means of crime. The following questions relate to strain theory:

5. Father attended college?
6. Father's occupation higher status?
13. He always tries hard?
20. Frustrated about the future?

A boy whose father attended college and has a higher status occupation will not be delinquent, according to strain theory, because he is not poor and deprived. He has a good chance of following in his father's footsteps, and thus can achieve the good things of life by legitimate means. But a boy who says "no" to these two questions may become delinquent. Having given up on a conventional career, the delinquent boy will not try hard in school and other conventional activities. The essence of strain theory is frustrated hopes, so the boy who is frustrated about the future should be delinquent.

NOTE: Question 20 ("Frustrated about the future?") produces strange results, just as similar questions do in Hirschi's research. You should know that correlations can lose validity if responses to a question are "highly skewed," that is if most boys give the same answer to the question and thus responses are very unbalanced. If hardly anybody is frustrated, how can frustration be a major cause of delinquency?

Finally, there is the hypothesis that religion makes boys be good, thus deterring delinquency. Both control theory and cultural deviance theory agree with this hypothesis, but each of these two approaches would want to say something about how religion has the power to influence individuals, and each might suggest some circumstances under which religion would lose this power [89]. Our two religion questions are:

10. Attends church often?
11. Believes God punishes our sins?

Projects

1. Explore the relationships between delinquency variables. Use Report Form 1 for this assignment. First, write your name and the date in the box in the upper right corner of the form. Select one of the schools, in Virginia or Washington, and check the appropriate box at the left top of the form. Below that write a four-digit random number, such as the four right-hand digits of a number taken from the telephone book. Now, give the computer commands to make it sample the school, using the random number.

After "Theory," near the top of the form, write "Do delinquency questions correlate?" The first three questions in the survey are about whether the boy is delinquent or not, and you are going to investigate whether the answers fit together. That is, do boys who have been picked up by the police admit that they have committed delinquent acts? Do boys who have been picked up by the police think of themselves as delinquents?

For your first analysis select question #2 to be variable X, and question #1 to be variable Y. Copy the table that appears on the computer screen onto the top part of Form 1. Write the two questions after "X" and "Y." Write the number of boys in each cell of the table on your computer screen, under "NO— Number" and "YES—Number." Then, press the "P" key to get the percents, and write them under "No— Percent" and "YES—Percent." Then press the "C" key to get Pearson's r and the statistical significance, writing them down where indicated on your data form. You can press the "C" key again, to get gamma and its statistical significance as well.

Finally, briefly answer the question, "What is the relationship between the variables?" Do they correlate significantly? If so, is it a positive correlation, or a negative one?

Now, do the same thing, using question #2 as variable X and question #3 as the Y variable. Use the bottom half of the data form for your results. You can now write a paragraph or two, stating whether kids who have been picked up by the police generally admit having committed delinquent acts and think of themselves as juvenile delinquents.

2. Select one of the three theories of delinquency (control, cultural, or strain) and test it. Your instructor could divide the class into three groups, one for each theory, and in a later class hold a debate over the results to see which theory has the most evidence in favor of it.

Which questions relate to your theory? Take a couple of pieces of lined paper, and write "1. Self-reported delinquent" at the top of one, and "2. Picked up by police" on the other. Now list the other questions you want to study, the ones that relate to your particular theory of deviance. For example, if you are investigating strain theory, which questions measure whether the boy is a victim of strain or not? Use *Experiments in Sociology* to find out the correlations (and their significances) linking each of the two delinquency questions to each of the ones relating to your theory. What are the relationships between the variables crucial to your theory and the two delinquency variables? What do they imply about the correctness of the theory?

After studying one school, you might want to repeat this research on the other school. We call this "replicating" research, to do it over again to see if you get the same results in a different social setting [82].

3. Explore the hypothesis that religion prevents delinquency, by doing two simulated questionnaire studies, one in Virginia and one in Washington state, focusing on questions #10 and #11. Check how the two correlate with each other, with the two delinquency questions, and with others you might be interested in. Do results of both studies support the hypothesis? How do the two states differ in terms of religion? In terms of delinquency?

2. BIRTHS, DEATHS, AND COHORTS

This simulation gives you a tiny society, the island of Microbora, and allows you to shape its demographic structure by experimenting with rates of birth (fertility) and death (mortality). The program can roughly simulate simple, traditional societies [253], preindustrial population trends [464], industrial societies [261], demographic transition [472], sudden declines [465], and population booms or explosions [486, 476].

A Trial Run

When the first set of decisions comes on the screen, it will ask, "Which kind of society would you like to experiment with?" Press the "5" key to select "Unrealistic test patterns." These are simple age and sex structures that a real society would not have, permitting us to examine the principles of the simulation in an uncomplicated way. The computer gives the choice of four test patterns. Select option #1, "Triangle."

The age and sex structure graph for the "Births, Deaths, and Cohorts" simulation will appear [464–465]. Up the left side are age ranges, from newborns 0 years of age up to the oldest folks, 99 years old. The screen is dominated by a triangle (or pyramid) composed of the letters "m" and "f." Each "m" represents a male inhabitant of Microbora, and each "f," a female. Opposite the age-range "55–59" stand just one "m" and one "f," indicating that only two inhabitants, one male and one female, are between 55 and 59 years old. At the base of the triangle, there are 12 males and 12 females under age 5.

Notice that some of the F's are capital letters, those representing women in the age groups from 15 through 44. These are the child-bearing years [460]. When the society starts having children, it will be these women who become mothers, and the number of children born will be the result of multiplying the birth rate times the number of women in this age bracket.

At various points in a simulation run, you may want to write down how many males and females there are in particular age groups. You can see the total number of members of both sexes displayed in the bright band at the top of the screen, and at the moment in this trial run you will find that there are 78 males and 78 females. You can learn the numbers in each age group by pressing the "T" key whenever the instructions at the bottom of the screen say, "Press T for table." Try it. A self-explanatory table will appear, giving you all the information you will generally need about the age and sex distribution of Microboran society. Now that you know how to get it, dismiss the table by pressing RETURN/ENTER.

You can make the computer record the demographic structure of Microboran society at various points in an experiment. You will get the information all at once at the end. Notice that the instructions at the bottom of the screen say, "Press... R to record data." Press the "R" key now. The instruction about R disappears, and "Records: 1" appears at the right side of the bright band near the bottom of the screen. This means you have recorded 1 demographic situation to see at the end. The computer can hold as many as 21 recordings, but will refuse to take any more beyond that.

The bright band near the bottom reads: "Fertility: 0, Mortality: 0." This indicates the birth and death instructions the simulation is currently set to work from. Just below the left of the lower bright band is "Fertility?" This asks you to give a new fertility instruction, but don't give it one. We want to stick with zero fertility and zero mortality for a while.

To get the simulation to run forward a step, press RETURN/ENTER once. Now, the bottom of the screen is asking you for a new mortality instruction, but don't give it one. Just press RETURN/ ENTER one more time. The triangle of males and females ripples and moves up a line. This represents everybody getting five years older. Nobody was born during these five years (zero fertility), and nobody died (zero mortality). So nothing changed but the ages.

Press "R" to record the new situation, then press RETURN/ENTER twice more to move everybody up another five years, and press "R" again. Now, let's make some babies. Notice again "Fertility?" in the lower left corner of the screen, a request for you to decide a birth rate. Press the "4" key, which will give you a medium birth rate. To avoid changing mortality at this point, press RETURN/ENTER once. In a flash, there will be 28 blessed events, 14 boy babies and 14 girl babies. These 28 are a birth cohort—those born in a particular five-year period [461]. Press "R" to register these births, and press RETURN/ENTER once quickly.

Now, let's experiment with mortality. Indeed, let's get really vicious and set a very high rate, by pressing the "8" key in response to the question, "Mortality?" Press "R," then look at the babies. A new cohort of kids has appeared in the 0–4 age range. But the first cohort, originally 28 strong, has been reduced by heavy infant mortality [326] to 20, now 5–9 years of age. Notice that the shape of the triangle above them is now distorted. We have especially lost some women in the child-bearing years and some older men.

One challenge in writing this simulation was to make it so that realistically complex things happened, but you did not have to give complex commands to get them. Whenever the mortality command is set high, infant mortality and deaths among women in the child-bearing years go way up. Also, except for the child-bearing years, men are less hardy than women, so their chances of living long are reduced. Women who make it through the child-bearing years, if their health was not broken by the traumas of motherhood, are apt to live longer than men.

If you look near the left end of the bright band at the top of the screen, you will see we have reached "Year 20," by five-year steps from the "Year 0" with which we began. To zip forward several years, keep pressing RETURN/ENTER until you hit Year 100. Microboran society is now in pretty bad shape, only 26 males and 23 females. Fertility is not high enough to offset mortality; there are fewer births than deaths. Keep pressing RETURN/ENTER until you hit Year 170. Everybody's gone, and Microbora is extinct.

Now press "S" to stop and get summary results. The screen fills with the first years you recorded, back at the beginning of the simulation, Year 0, Year 5, and Year 10. Remember that we started without births and deaths, simply letting the Microborans get older. That's what the table shows happening over the first ten years. You can press RETURN/ENTER to see more data, the next set of years you recorded.

Instructions on the screen will tell you how to proceed in getting more results. After the age and sex statistics for recorded years, there will be a table of summary statistics. Then you will see a table of fertility and mortality commands, along with a rough graph of the total population over the course of the simulation run.

A technical comment on the fertility and mortality commands is necessary [459–461]. When asked "Fertility?" or "Mortality?" you may press any number key from zero through nine (0–9). Zero really does mean a birth rate or death rate of zero. But the other numbers are just commands. The program contains secret formulas that turn these simple commands into appropriate rates. Advanced students are invited to try to decode the commands and figure out what rates they produce, but they should be warned that the mortality commands give different death rates for the two sexes and twenty age groups, just as a real society would experience.

If you set fertility high but mortality low, Microbora will experience a population explosion. The island will get stuffed with people, and there may not be room on the screen to display all the "m" and "f" inhabitants in the younger age groups. I built a little warning signal into the program to let you know when there is not room to show everybody in the graph. A letter will appear on the left between the age group numbers and the first "m." If the letter is an "M," it means there is an overflow of males. An "F" means an overflow of females, and "B" means there are too many of both sexes to display on the screen. Check the table, by pressing the T key, to see how many.

Projects

1. Experiment with population explosions in traditional and transitional societies [440, 469, 476], using Report Form 2 to record your data. At the bottom of the form, where it says "Experiment 1 began with which type of society?" write "traditional" and begin a run of the simulation, selecting "Traditional society." In the top part of the form, labeled "Experiment 1," write the number of males and females in the society for Year 0. Then press "T" to get the table so you can write in the percentages of the population in each of the three age groups. Then press RETURN/ ENTER to return to the graph.

Keep writing down results as you run through the simulation up to Year 200, but change fertility and mortality numbers as follows, writing the new commands for the year you change them. Year 0: 8,6; Year 5: 8,5; Year 10: 8,4; Year 15: 8,3; Year 20: 8,2. Keep at 8,2 for a long time, and then make these changes: Year 100: 7,2; Year 105: 6,2; Year 110: 5,2; Year 115: 4,2; Year 120: 3,2. This sequence represents what might happen as a traditional society is radically transformed by modern medicine [477]. First, the death rate goes down as many diseases are conquered. The birth rate stays high for a time because of cultural lag [437, 478], until it, too, begins to drop. At the beginning, there is a stable population with high birth and death rates. Then there is a long period in which the death rate drops faster than the birth rate, and the result is population explosion. To simulate the full demographic transition, you bring the birth rate down again at the end [473].

Experiment 2: run the simulation for "transitional" society, recording what happens, without making changes in the birth and death rates. This shows that if a society stays in a transitional condition, with fertility only somewhat higher than mortality, it still experiences a population explosion, although a more gentle one. Indeed, both societies finish the experiments with continuing growth, even if not so explosive as during the first century of the traditional society. This reminds us that demographic transition theory may not, in fact, give us the confidence to predict an end to population growth as developing nations become technologically modern.

2. Examine the phenomenon of a "baby boom," in which fertility rises very high for a brief period [486–491]. To get the idea, first run the simulation for the test pattern called "Inverted T," without changing commands. This unrealistic pattern shows how a very large birth cohort flows through the age structure. Notice that when the bulge of boom babies reaches the child-bearing years, a second baby boom is caused by the fact that now there is an unusually high number of potential mothers. The second boom spreads out over more years than the first, and you can even see traces of a third boom when these second-boom babies become parents.

For both of the experiments you write down, select "post-industrial society." In the first, start with fertility = 9, mortality = 2. After the first boom cohort of babies, keep both fertility and mortality set at 2, writing down the population statistics for the years listed in the report form. For the second experiment, start with fertility and mortality at 2, and do not change it throughout the run. When you compare the populations for Year 200, you will see that the effect of the one big cohort of babies in Experiment 1 persists long after they have died of old age.

3. WORLD POPULATION TRENDS

This program lets you trace the rise and fall of the populations of twenty-five nations of the world—plus five more nations you can invent or look up in the library. It contains real census estimates of how many people lived in each of the twenty-five nations every ten years from 1900 through 1980. And it gives you the power to project how big each nation might be in future years, following a wide range of assumptions [cf. 461–462, 468–469, 475, 480].

A Trial Run

To get practice with this program, let's experiment with the United States. Once you select "World Population Trends," the computer will display a list of countries and ask "Which nations would you like to study?" Read the instructions on the computer screen so they will be familiar to you next time. Then type in the number 25, selecting the U.S.A. Next press the RETURN/ENTER key. Notice that a bright box lights up in front of "U.S.A" on the screen, announcing that you have chosen this nation. You could go on to choose four more nations, but let's stick with just this one. So press the "S" key to stop selecting nations. Now, the computer asks what year to begin its analysis. Press the zero key (not to be confused with the letter Oh) to start with 1900.

A simple table will flash on the screen, telling you that the population of the U.S.A. was 76 million in 1900, and that the annual rate of growth was 1.93 percent. This means that the population increased at a rate of 1.93 percent on average in every year from 1900 to 1910. How much would that add up to over the decade? Press RETURN/ENTER to find out.

A new heading appears at the right of the table, "1910 Population," and the number 92 appears twice below it. The first 92 is the computer's projection that the population would grow from 76 million to 92 million, if the annual growth rate was 1.93 percent [458–460]. The second 92, between two arrowheads (">92<"), is the actual U.S. population as counted by the 1910 census.

The beginning of the century was a time of especially rapid growth for America, with lots of babies being born and immigrants arriving on the U.S. shores [32]. Later decades, such as the Depression years of the 1930s, showed much slower growth. How big would the population be if the explosive growth from 1900 to 1910 continued unabated right up until today?

Press RETURN/ENTER, see what changes, then press RETURN/ENTER again, to get a projection of America's population in 1920. If the growth rate had stayed at 1.93 percent a year, the population would be 111.4 million in 1920, but the actual 1920 census found only 105.7 people in the nation. Obviously, the nation's growth must have slowed a bit in the 1910–1920 decade, because our projection is too high.

Now press RETURN/ENTER several more times, looking at what happens each time you do, until you get up to 1980. If the growth rate had stayed at the high level of 1900, there would be 350.7 million Americans in 1980, much more than the 226.5 million actually counted by the 1980 census. This discrepancy of fully 124.2 million does not indicate that our computer program is silly. Instead, it shows what great changes have occurred in America. The birth rate has dropped tremendously, and federal laws have greatly damped immigration. As you experiment with this simulation, think over the possible meaning of the often surprising results you find.

Press RETURN/ENTER a couple of times, until you get the estimate for 1990. Now there is no number in arrowheads at the right, because we do not know what the 1990 census results will be. Press RETURN/ENTER again a couple of times to get the projected population in 2000 if the 1900 growth rate had held up all century: 514 million people!

Look at the bottom of the screen. If it says just "Press RETURN" or "Press ENTER," then do so. Now the bottom of the screen should say, "Press RETURN/ENTER to go on, or S to stop. To change basic decisions, press D." Don't worry about the decisions yet. Just press the S key to stop so we can start over.

Now select choice #1 to start over, still working with the U.S.A. The computer asks you what year you want to begin with. Select 1970 by pressing the "7" key. In a second you will see that the population was 203.3 million in 1970, and that the annual growth rate from 1970 to 1980 was 1.09 percent, rather than the 1.93 it was in 1900–1910.

Press RETURN/ENTER to get the 1980 population. The computer's projection is 226.6, and the actual census got 226.5; this difference is just a tiny error in rounding off the calculations, not a real discrepancy, and you should ignore differences like this. Press RETURN/ENTER a few more times until you get the population projection for the year 2000. This time it should be 281.4 million, much lower than the 514 million people who would inhabit the country if the 1900–1910 growth rate had held up.

Now you know how to run a simple projection. You can select a nation, or as many as five to study simultaneously, and you can decide what year the projections should begin. In the following section you will learn how to make five different decisions about how the projections should be done, and even work with new data—real or imaginary—you can type into the computer.

Five Decisions

Select some nations to work with, and a year to start in. Then the table will appear on the screen with the words "To change basic decisions, press D" at the bottom. Do press D. The table will vanish to be replaced by a screen full of instructions. You have five decisions to make, each one with two choices.

Five bright boxes, with words inside, are numbered from 1 to 5. The first says, "DISPLAY ACTUAL CENSUS FIGURES WHEN AVAILABLE." This is the decision that puts the numbers inside arrowheads, the actual census results, on the screen, Decision 1. To change it, press the "1" key. Suddenly, the bright box will move over to the other alternative, "DO NOT DISPLAY ACTUAL CENSUS FIGURES." If you leave it like this, numbers in arrowheads will never appear on the screen. To change Decision 1 back, press "1" again.

Try changing the other decisions back and forth, by typing numbers from "2" through "5." Don't type very fast, because the computer has to think about each change and would miss some of your commands. The full set of decisions will stay on the screen until you have all five just the way you want them. Then you press RETURN/ENTER to get back to the table. In our trial run, above, all five decisions were made with the left-hand alternative. More complicated things happen when you choose some of the right-hand alternatives. We have explained Decision 1. Here are what the other four do:

Decision 2: If you choose "PROJECTIONS FROM RATES YOU TYPE IN," you get to add your own growth rates to those calculated by the computer and compare the results of projections using both sets. If you choose to do this, bright rectangles will appear in parentheses for each nation in turn. This is where you will type a new growth rate for that nation. It should be a number like 1.25 or .88. The computer wants two digits after the decimal point, and won't take any more than that. So you can't type 1.667, just 1.67. If you want 1.5, type 1.50. You may use negative growth rates, like −.06 or −2.13, representing a decrease in population each year. Also, the computer won't accept very big rates of change, anything more than ±9.99. Both your growth rates and population projections based on them will appear in parentheses.

Decision 3: This decision is a bit subtle, but it produces marvelous results, so it is very much worth while learning. So far, the projections have stuck with the same growth rate year after year. But we know that growth rates can change. Suppose the growth rate is 3 percent a year from 1900 to 1910, and 2 percent a year from 1910 to 1920. What might you guess it could be from 1920 to 1930? Maybe there is a trend in the growth rate. First it was 3, then it was 2, so it might be 1, next. A rate of 1 percent would be reasonable for 1920 to 1930. Perhaps next it will be 0, and after that maybe −1, dropping by 1 percentage point each decade.

The normal choice for Decision 3 is "TRENDS BASED ON ONE DECADE ONLY." If you select "TRENDS BASED ON CHANGES OVER TWO DECADES," then the basic projections (not in parentheses) will be based on changing rates. If the rate of growth was increasing over the first two decades in your run, then it will keep on increasing at the same speed. Not only will the population rise, but it will also rise faster and faster as the growth rate goes up.

Decision 4: You may want to experiment with your own system of changing growth rates. If so, you can choose the option under Decision 4 to "SELECT A GROWTH RATE FOR EACH TIME INTERVAL." This means you type in new growth rates (using the bright rectangles in parentheses) for every single year, so it can get tedious if you have no good reason to do it. Of course, this decision is not relevant unless you have also made the right-hand choice for Decision 2 and thus do plan to type in new rates.

Decision 5: Our data on populations from 1900 to 1980 are for years ending in zero, and so the simulation starts out assuming you want to study population change over intervals of a decade. But suppose you want to select a new interval. Perhaps you want to estimate the population of a country for a year like 1965. To do this, start the program for the census year (ending in zero) immediately before the year you want to study. For 1965, you'd pick 1960. Choose the right-hand alternative for Decision 5. Then press RETURN/ENTER to get back to the table, and press RETURN/ENTER again to go on. Now, the bottom of the screen tells you how to change the interval from 10 to any other number of years, from 1 to 99. Pick 5 years and you'll get right to 1965.

NOTE: If you change the interval away from the 10 years the computer starts with, you cannot use the second alternative for Decision 3, "TRENDS BASED ON CHANGES OVER TWO DECADES," because you are asking the computer to think in terms of decades with one decision, and something other than decades with the other. This won't drive the computer crazy, but it is likely to produce crazy, useless results. What's worse—the results won't look crazy enough for you to be suspicious of them. They'll just be wrong.

Other Nations

You can input your own population statistics for real or imaginary nations, and produce projections for them with all the options available for the twenty-five nations built into the program. Start the program and look over the list of nations that appears at the beginning. You will see that nations numbered 26 through 30 are called "New #1," "New #2," etc. Select New #1 by typing its number (26) and pressing RETURN/ENTER. Then press "S" to stop selecting.

The screen will show a new instruction asking you to type in the population of New #1 for the year 1900. NOTE: Type in the full population, not an abbreviated form. For example, in 1900 you should type in 76,000,000 for the U.S.A., not just 76. You may use commas in the number, or not, as you prefer. After typing the 1900 population, press RETURN/ENTER. Now "1910" appears, and you should type in the population for that year. The computer would get confused by very small or very big populations, so don't give it numbers less than 100,000 or bigger than a few billion. If you want to study populations under 100,000, simply add 3 zeroes at the end of each (e.g., 1,000 becomes 1,000,000) and the computer will display populations in thousands, rather than millions (e.g., "76" would represent 76,000, rather than 76,000,000)

Continue doing this through 1980, and the computer will ask, "Is all this information correct?" Look over the nine population figures to make sure they are right, and press "Y" for Yes if they all are. If you see an error, you can press "N" for No and get a chance to retype all the numbers. If you decide to study more than one NEW nation, you will have to keep track of which is which.

WARNING: If you type in very unrealistic numbers, or if there are drastic leaps in the population, you may get false results, and it is even possible the program will "crash" as the computer gives up on the calculations you have asked it to do. I wrote the program to handle most strange things you might do, but if I had made errors absolutely impossible I would have prevented you from doing valid experiments you might invent. At the very worst, you'll have to start the disk over from scratch. But be alert for impossible results, when you are using very unusual data.

Unless you invent imaginary census figures, it is very hard to get numbers for the NEW nations. Most less developed nations never had a census until 1950 or after, and their population estimates are unreliable. Also, countries hold their censuses in various different years. The most recent U.S. census was in 1980, but Canada held one in 1981. I had to work for many hours to calculate decent population estimates for years ending in zero for twenty-five nations, and frankly some of them are rather uncertain.

Consider the United Kingdom, for example, a nation with a long tradition of excellent censuses. There was a census in 1931, and another in 1951, but none in the dark war days of 1941. Another example is India, which underwent partition into three nations: India, Bangladesh, and Pakistan. For comparability over time, I have combined the three here as "India+." Because of economic, social, and political conditions, the figures for Indonesia and Nigeria are particularly unreliable.

Projects

1. Select one of the 25 nations listed in the program and do four projections of its population up through the year 2100. Write the name of the nation you will study in the box labeled "nation" in the upper left corner of Report Form 3. In the first run, start with the year 1900 so that the computer will use the growth rate from 1900 to 1910 to project the population for all the later dates. Write the population projections for each decade starting with 1950 in the first column of the report form.

The second run should start with the year 1950, so that the projections will all be based on the growth rate from 1950 to 1960. These population projections should go in the second column of the form. The third run should be done just the same way, except that you will begin with 1970, and you will not have population estimates to write down for 1950 and 1960.

For the fourth and last run projecting the nation's population, choose 1970 again, but this time press "D" as soon as appropriate to get the list of five decisions on the screen. Change Decision 3 to get "TRENDS BASED ON CHANGES OVER TWO DECADES." This means that the growth rate will change from decade to decade, continuing the trend in rates of the two decades 1960–1970 and 1970–1980.

2. After World War II, Germany was divided into two nations, the Federal Republic (West Germany) and the People's Republic (East Germany). These two nations have the same cultural heritage, but live under very different political systems. West Germany has a free or "capitalist" economy, while East Germany has a centrally controlled or "communist" economy. Study population trends for these two Germanies to see if the difference in their systems of government has a clear impact on their demographic history and future.

The results of this study may surprise you. Because the boundaries of Germany changed drastically over the first half of the twentieth century, we have not included it among our 25 nations. But the table below gives population estimates for the decades after the war, so you can use two of the extra nations, "26 New #1" and "27 New #2" to input these data. Because you do not have figures for 1900 to 1940, type zeros for these years. Remember that you did this so you won't ask the computer to figure growth rates for decades you don't have data about.

YEAR	WEST GERMANY	EAST GERMANY
1950	49,986,000	18,388,000
1960	55,433,000	17,058,000
1970	60,714,000	17,070,000
1980	61,174,000	16,797,000

3. Following the directions of Project 1, or using your own approach, study population growth for one of the American states or Canadian provinces. Any almanac will have state census figures for each decade, and Canadian census figures are also readily available. Canada holds its main census in years ending

198

in "1" (1971, 1981, etc.) but you don't have to go through the lengthy process of estimating the population for years ending in zero, as I have done for the 25 nations. Simply type in the statistics one year off (1971 for 1970) and remember to add 1 to any year the computer displays.

4. A SURVEY OF YOU AND YOUR FRIENDS _____

This program contains a 45-item questionnaire that you can administer to as many as five people, right on the computer. It illustrates how questionnaire *scales* (or *indexes*) are created by combining responses to several questions. But it also lets you and four of your friends discover how different your opinions are—which of you are most similar and which are most different. With one exception, the books and articles from which I took the scales are listed in Stark's bibliography and play important roles in his text.

A Trial Run_____

The survey program begins with a menu of five options, and you should press the "1" key to select "Administer the survey." Now the computer asks, "Which sections do you want in the survey?" There are three sections, on three different topics: religion, delinquency, and academic subjects. For this trial run, press the "7" key to get all three.

Immediately, the computer will ask you the first of the religion questions, inquiring about your beliefs concerning God. Right now, don't worry about expressing your true question. Just look the question over to become familiar with it, and press the "1" key. Continue through the other questions, always pressing the "1" key. If you press the wrong key by mistake, you can usually back up and get a second chance to press the correct key by pressing "B" (for Back up) in response to the next question.

After 9 religion questions, in a variety of formats, will come 6 questions about possible delinquent acts you might have performed. For purposes of this trial run, keep pressing the "1" key, professing complete innocence. After these questions about minor crimes comes a set of 30 questions about academic subjects, courses you might have taken in school. "On a scale of 1 to 7, how much do you like Botany?" Again, press the "1" key each time, until you complete the survey and find yourself back at the main menu of this program.

Now you have the option to analyze the results, so do so. Press the "2" key to see a brief analysis of your responses to the survey, a table of "index scores from the questionnaire." You see eight scales listed: Orthodoxy, Particularism, Religiosity, Delinquency, Male subjects, Sciences, Humanities, and Academic. Below, I will explain what each of the scales means and show you how it was calculated from your responses to several questions.

For now, note that you got a score of 3 on the Orthodoxy index, as indicated in the upper half of the table on your computer screen. The lower half, labeled "Percentages," shows that these 3 points were 75 percent of a perfect score on the Orthodoxy index. That is, a score of 3 points means that a person is about 75 percent orthodox in their religious beliefs, according to a sociological conception of Orthodoxy we will consider shortly.

You scored 6 points on the Particularism Index, which equals a 100 percent score on that index. But you scored 0 points on Delinquency, which is the same as a 0 percent score. Remember that you claimed to be innocent of any wrongdoing, pressing the "1" key in response to the 6 delinquency questions, so perhaps a zero score makes sense even without a deep discussion of how the Delinquency index is created.

Now press RETURN/ENTER, and get back to the main menu. Administer the questionnaire one more time, by pressing the "1" key. This time, the computer does not ask you which sections to include in the survey. It will continue with the decision you made last time.

Go through the whole questionnaire again, but this time press the "3" key in response to each question. When you get back to the main menu, press "2" to analyze the results.

Now Table 1 shows the scores of two people, Person A and Person B. Of course, Person A is you, the first time you answered all the questions, and Person B is your second set of answers. Notice that Person B scores much lower on Orthodoxy and Particularism, and much higher on Delinquency, than does Person A.

Press RETURN/ENTER, and you get a further analysis that was not possible when you had only one respondent. Table 2 shows how *different* the two respondents were (A versus B). A 0 percent would mean the two got the same score on the particular index, while 100 percent would mean they scored as differently as they possibly could. Once you know what the indexes mean, you can read this table to see in what ways your two respondents are very different, and in what ways less different or even identical.

Press RETURN/ENTER again, and you get a rather small table with only one number in it, expressing how different on average the two individuals' responses to the 30 academic subjects were. Another press of RETURN/ENTER takes you back to the main menu. Now that you know how to run the program, you must be intrigued by what the results mean. To understand that, we must look at each of the scales, in turn, and in the following three sections we will consider the three separate sections of the questionnaire. You might want to follow along on the computer screen, looking at the specific questions as I explain them for you.

Religion Questions

The first four questions in the religion section were used by Glock and Stark (*Christian Beliefs and Anti-Semitism,* New York: Harper and Row, 1966) to produce a scale of Christian Orthodoxy, and we will make an Orthodoxy scale from them, using the same approach [366]. The word "orthodox" means strict adherence to an established religious standard. Many denominations use the word in their names, particularly the Eastern Orthodox churches, including Greek Orthodox, Russian Orthodox, and Ukranian Orthodox. Obviously, Orthodox Jews have somewhat different beliefs and practices than do Orthodox Christians.

The Glock and Stark Orthodoxy scale does not refer to Eastern Orthodox churches, but to a widespread tradition in American religion. When a social scientist names a questionnaire scale, he or she defines a particular concept, and it would be a mistake to use other definitions while studying his or her work. Glock and Stark based their scale on a deep understanding of American religious history, but perhaps the best way to understand their concept of Orthodoxy is to see how they coded and combined our first four questionnaire items to measure it. (The table on page 366 of Stark's text refers to a 3-item Orthodoxy scale, used in a national survey where there was a limit on how many questions they could afford, while our program is based on the 4-item scale in their original study done only in California.)

The first question, about the existence of God, gives respondents many common opinions to choose from. But the traditional response for devout believers was, "I know God really exists and I have no doubts about it." If a respondent selects this one, he or she is given one point on the Orthodoxy index. Obviously, members of non-Christian religions may hold this view of God, but it is interesting to note that many people who consider themselves good Christians do not. Among the 151 Congregationalists who responded to the Glock and Stark survey, only 41 percent gave this response, while 38 percent expressed definite doubts.

The second question focuses on Christian orthodoxy, because it measures belief in the divinity of Jesus. A respondent gets 1 point on the Orthodoxy scale for answering, "Jesus is the Divine Son of God and I have no doubts about it."

The third item is about Biblical miracles, and Christians are not the only people who might give the Orthodox response: "I believe the miracles happened, just as the Bible says they did." Again, this reponse gives the person 1 Orthodoxy point. Notice that this is response number 4 to the Biblical miracles item in our survey, while the Orthodox responses to the first two questions required the respondent to press the "1" key.

The fourth and final item in the Orthodoxy index concerns Satan, and the person gets 1 point for saying, "Completely true" in response to the statement "The Devil actually exists."

To see where a respondent stands on the Orthodoxy scale, add together the points they got on these four questions. Somebody who gives the orthodox response for all four items will have a total of 4 points, and the lowest possible score is 0 points.

Of course, each question is of interest in itself. For a different study, we might be especially interested in people who believe in a higher power, but not in a personal God, and who think Jesus was only a man. Some of these people will feel they are quite religious, but obviously their religion is of a very different kind from that identified by the Orthodoxy index. In real research studies, we often analyze data several ways around. Our educational purpose right now is to see how indexes are created and how they tap dimensions along which people may vary.

Glock and Stark used a second important religion scale they called the Particularism index. As they define it, "religious particularism is the belief that only one's own religion is legitimate. . . . To the particularistic mind there are not faiths, but one true faith" (Glock and Stark, 1966:20). Orthodoxy refers to a traditional standard of belief, but many orthodox believers may be very tolerant of other faiths and hold friendly feelings for people who happen to disagree with them [cf. 288]. Particularism adds an element of hostility toward other religions, and certainly implies the conviction that one belongs to God's chosen people. Almost every denomination in every religious tradition contains some people who feel this way, but Glock and Stark found that Orthodoxy and Particularism tended to go together.

The Particularism index is made up out of responses to three questions about the religious concept of salvation, and like the Orthodoxy index it mainly measures a person's attitudes toward traditional Christian issues. The first and third items are about Jesus, again. How necessary for salvation is belief in Jesus Christ as Savior? Would being ignorant of Jesus prevent one from gaining salvation? Notice these two items are phrased in opposite ways; the first is about what one needs to gain salvation, while the second is about what might prevent salvation.

The remaining Particularism item, placed between the two about Jesus in our survey, is: "How necessary for salvation is being a member of your particular religious faith?" There are three possible responses to each Particularism item. Response number 1 indicates an absolute necessity for salvation, while number 2 indicates a possible connection with salvation. The third response suggests no strong belief about what might be necessary for salvation. A respondent gets 2 points on the Particularism index for each strong "1" response, and 1 point for each milder "2" response. Somebody who responded by pressing the "3" key would get 0 points. Thus, the possible scores on the Particularism index range from 0 up through 6.

Compare these two religion indexes, for a moment, in terms of how the points were counted. For Orthodoxy, a person got 1 point for the completely traditional response to each question, and no points for any of the other alternatives. For Particularism, a person got 2 points for a strong response and 1 point for a weaker response.

After the seven items of the two indexes Glock and Stark used in their famous 1966 study, I have included two other religion items that Stark also used in his later research with Travis Hirschi and with me.

201

One asks how frequently a person attends religious services, while the other gets the person's opinion about life after death.

Just to show how indexes can be put together, and not with any serious research purpose, our program makes a big Religiosity index by combining the Orthodoxy index, the Particularism index, and these two other questions. To create it, the computer first adds together the two indexes. A person could score from 0 through 4 on Orthodoxy, and from 0 through 6 on Particularism. So he or she could score from zero through 10 on the two indexes added together.

The question about how often the person attends religious services has six responses, from 1 (never) through 6 (once a week or more). So, if we add it to Orthodoxy and Particularism, we get a scale that goes from 1 through 16. The final item asks for an opinion on the statement, "There is a life beyond death." The possible responses range from 1 (strongly disagree) through 5 (strongly agree). If we add this one in, too, we get a scale that goes from 2 through 21. But, we'd like a scale that starts with zero for people who show no religious tendencies at all by these measures. So the final Religiosity index is created by subtracting 2 at the end: Orthodoxy + Particularism + attendance at religious services + agreement with life beyond death - 2. By subtracting the 2 points from everybody's Religiosity total, we get an index that ranges from 0 points up through 19.

Now, I must stress that Religiosity is a real hodgepodge as indexes go. It gives a lot of weight to frequency of church attendance, as many as 5 points from that question alone, and not so much weight to the first four questions, which can contribute only 1 point each. Social scientists, like Glock and Stark, go to great lengths to make sure their indexes are constructed as well as possible. For example, they correlated Orthodoxy and Particularism with many other items in the questionnaire to make sure that the patterns were entirely reasonable. Our Religiosity index is merely meant to show how we can combine items in different ways to make an index, although it does have the merit of being based on a broad set of questions about traditional American religion.

I am sure many of you will feel that your own religious views are not completely captured by our nine questions. Certainly this will be true if you don't happen to be Christian, but many Christians will have this reaction, too. Just remember that, like all good sociological scales, the Glock–Stark Orthodoxy and Particularism idexes were created with a very definite scientific purpose in mind, drawing upon a clear sociological theory, and aimed at the church members who were the respondents to their study.

Delinquency Questions

The six delinquency items were created by Travis Hirschi (*Causes of Delinquency*, Berkeley: University of California Press, 1969) and used by Hirschi and Stark ("Hellfire and Delinquency," *Social Problems* 17(1969):202–213) in their journal article on the connection between religion and behavior [89–91]. As you will see on the computer screen, the questions ask whether the person has ever done a particular delinquent act, and there are four possible answers to each: (1) No, never; (2) More than a year ago; (3) During the last year; (4) During the last year AND more than a year ago.

In his original study, Hirschi (1969:62) created several different indexes by giving different numbers of points for different answers. For example, he created a "Recency" index that measured whether the person had been delinquent during the last year. A respondent got 1 point for answer 3 or answer 4, since both of these indicate that the person did the delinquent act in the last year. Performing the deviant act only before the past year (response number 2) was not counted in the Recency index.

Our Delinquency index was Hirschi's "Standard" index. I chose this one simply because few of you might get much of a delinquency score if we restricted ourselves to just the past year. We give the person one point for a 2, 3, or 4 response—for ever having performed the deviant act. This produces a scale that goes from 0 points, if the person says he or she never did any of the six acts, up to 6 points, if the person performed each of the acts at some time in the past.

Academic Questions

The 30 academic questions produce four overlapping indexes. The first is called Male subjects and was one that criminologist Robert Crutchfield [187] and I created for an essay we published on sex role ideology [160–165] and delinquency ("Sex Role Ideology and Delinquency," *Sociological Perspectives* 26 (1983):253–274). Our survey of 862 college students already included a standard psychological scale that was supposed to measure the respondent's attitudes toward "traditional" or "liberated" sex roles, but it seemed to us that its questions were very hypothetical, few of the items having much to do with college students' daily lives. So we created a second sex-roles index out of students' preferences for eight academic subjects, under the assumption that students' ratings of different subjects they might have spent months taking really would say something important about the respondents.

Four subjects were given much higher ratings by men, on average, than by women: physics, engineering, astronomy, and economics. Four others were preferred by women: social work, a foreign language, literature, and art. To be sure, many women like economics, and men may like art. But the responses of 862 students identified the first four fields as predominantly male, and the second four as female. Because males are more often guilty of delinquent acts, we wanted a Male subjects index to use in our analysis of the possible effect of sex roles on deviant behavior.

Each of the academic subjects is rated on a scale of 1 through 7. To make the index, we add the scores for the four male subjects, subtract the scores for the four female subjects, then add 24. This gives a Male subjects index that ranges from 0 through 48.

To make sure you understand, consider the extremes. Suppose a person hated all the male subjects, giving each a "1" response. That's 4 points to start with. Then the person loves the female subjects, giving each a "7." That means you subtract 28 from 4, because you are supposed to subtract each of the female-subject scores (in this example 7 for each). That gives –24. Finally you add 24, which brings you up to 0. Thus, hating the male subjects and loving the female subjects gives you a 0 score on the Male subjects index.

But suppose you loved the male subjects and hated all the female ones. Then you would have 28 points for the male ones, minus 4 points for the female ones, which equals 24. Then you add the 24 points the instructions call for, and get a total of 48. This is the extreme high score on the Male subjects index. Of course, there is nothing morally or intellectually good (or bad) about getting a high score. The index is a scientific measurement tool, not a test of good judgment. And if our research purpose had been different, we might have put the numbers together in a different way to create a Female subjects index.

After the work with Crutchfield, when the dataset had grown to include fully 1465 respondents from the University of Washington, I analyzed the academic preferences further. The questionnaire included two items that are not in our present survey: How much does the person like the sciences, in general? How much does the person like the humanities, in general? Well, which of the 30 subjects are sciences, and which are humanities? Rather than puzzle this out in my own opinions, I looked at the correlations linking these two items with the 30.

The correlation between liking the sciences and liking chemistry was 0.64, a very high number. In contrast, the correlation between liking the humanities and liking chemistry is –0.04. Surely, chemistry is one of the sciences. There were 12 fields that correlated 0.30 or greater with the sciences, in descending order: chemistry, biology, physics, zoology, medicine, engineering, oceanography, mathematics, botany, astronomy, geology, and architecture. Eight of the fields are clearly sciences, while mathematics is essential for the sciences, and medicine, engineering, and architecture make use of scientific findings and methods of analysis.

The Sciences index was created by adding together all the responses for these 12 items and subtracting 12 from the result. This scale ranges from 0 through 72.

As luck would have it, exactly 12 other subjects correlated at 0.30 or above with the humanities. Literature was the highest, at 0.60, and the twelve, in descending order, are: literature, classics (ancient civilization), history, social work, drama, art, a foreign language, communications, anthropology, music, education, and psychology. Sociologists shouldn't snicker to see psychology classed among the humanities rather than the sciences, because sociology wound up in neither of these indexes. In fact, sociology was closer to the humanities (0.29) than to the sciences (−0.01).

The Humanities index was created the same way as the Sciences index. Add together the 12 responses, and subtract 12, getting an index that goes from 0 through 72.

Notice that these two indexes are completely distinct from each other. There is no questionnaire item used in both. However, both of them overlap the Male subjects index, because male respondents tended to rate the sciences higher than did women, while female respondents rated the humanities higher than did men.

The final Academic index simply combines all the academic subjects. Add the 30 responses together, and subtract 30. The Academic index runs from 0 through 180. I suppose it measures how much the individual likes college.

Understanding Your Results

Each of these eight indexes can be used separately in a research study, but as they stand it is a little hard to compare them with each other, because their ranges are so very different. The highest score on the Orthodoxy index is 4, but the highest score on the Academic index is 180. Therefore, the bottom part of Table 1 makes the indexes comparable by translating them into percentages. The calculation is simple. Divide the person's score by the highest possible score for the index, then multiply by 100 to get percent.

If you scored 0 on any index, then your percent of the highest possible score is 0 percent. However, if you got the highest possible score, for example, 4 on Orthodoxy, then your percentage is 100 percent. A person who scored 90 on the Academic index would get 50 percent, because 90 is 50 percent of 180, the highest possible score for this index.

Table 2 shows how different Person A is from Person B on each index whose questions they answered. If more than two persons responded to the survey, each possible pair is compared. A person who scored 0 percent on a given index is 100 percent different from someone who scored 100 percent. What about two people who scored 40 percent and 60 percent on a given index? They are 20 percent different.

Table 3 offers a little different twist on the academic questions. The computer goes through all the responses to academic questions from Person A and Person B, comparing them. For each question, it counts the difference in the responses. If Person A pressed the "1" key, and Person B pressed "3," the computer subtracts 1 from 3 and finds that the respondents were two ($3 - 1 = 2$) points apart on this question. The machine adds up the differences for all 30 academic questions. If, as in our trial run, they are 2 points apart on each, the computer gets a total of 60 points different ($2 \times 30 = 60$).

The total possible difference is 180 points. This is true because the greates possible disagreement on any one subject is 6 ($7 - 1 = 6$), and there are 30 questions ($6 \times 30 = 180$). So if Person A and Person B are 60 points apart on academic subjects, they show 33 percent of the total possible difference (60/180 = 1/3 = about 33 percent).

Notice that this compares the respondents' college preferences in a way very different from the Academic index. Table 3 shows the total disagreement about particular subjects. The Academic index simply compares how much the two people differ in their average liking for college courses.

Consider two people, C and D. Let's say Person C loves the first 15 subjects (giving them all "7" responses) and hates the last 15 ("1" responses). Person D, in contrast, hates the first 15 ("1" responses) and loves the last 15 ("7" responses). On average, each likes school just as much, and they will have exactly the same scores on the Academic index—90 points or 50 percent. Thus, the difference between them is 0 percent, as Table 2 would show if you were analyzing them on your computer. But Table 3 would show a 100 percent difference between them, because every subject Person C loves D hates, and vice versa.

Projects

1. Select five "characters" from the Stark text, and play the role of each one while responding to the religion questions in our survey. By a character I mean a particular type of person as Stark describes him or her in his book. For example, Person A might be a Jewish immigrant to the United States, and Person B might be an Italian immigrant. Study each character, as described by Stark, and using all the information at your disposal, imagine how each one would respond to the religion survey. Keeping track of which person is which, and writing down your responses to the questions, type each character's likely responses into the computer.

Report Form 4 can be used to copy data from Table 1 and Table 2. You should attach to your result a comment on why the results came out as they did—why the five characters responded in the way they did to the survey and how the indexes summarized their responses.

2. With four of your friends or classmates, take the full 45-item survey as honestly as you can. Make sure each person understands all of the questions, for example, understanding that the last 30 ask them to express their preferences for 30 academic subjects, courses they might take in college. But you should not discuss or think about the ways these separate questions will be turned into indexes. Just respond to each question as accurately as possible.

When all five have answered the questions, write down the results from Table 1, Table 2, and Table 3, using Report Form 4. Now sit down, all five of you, and discuss the meaning of the indexes. In particular, do you think each of them helped you understand how you were similar or different in that area of your opinions and actions? That is, do you think each index was a reasonably valid [16] measure of the particular aspect of the respondents?

5. BOSTON'S NORTHWEST END

Years ago, William Foote White studied Boston's Italian North End (*Street Corner Society*, Chicago: University of Chicago Press, 1955) and Herbert Gans studied a less well organized poor section, Boston's West End (*Urban Villagers*, New York: Free Press, 1962). Both sections of the city became threatened by "urban renewal," the plan to tear down the cheap if blighted housing in them and replace it with more expensive, nicer buildings. The residents of the North End were able to get together to block this plan, and their section of the city lives today as a famous and beloved landmark to the heritage of Italian-Americans. Although some tried, the residents of the West End failed to get together to block the bulldozers, and their neighborhood was scraped away to ground level, later replaced by high-income apartments.

As reported in Professor Stark's text, sociologist Mark Granovetter has explained the success of the North End and the failure of the West End in terms of the network of social relationships that existed in the neighborhood [559]. To grow, a social movement has to spread from person to person, and people are much more likely to join if they have close friends who are already members. This simulation lets you experiment with a hypothetical Northwest End of Boston, where you can decide the social characteristics of the neighborhood and see how quickly or slowly a movement can spread.

A Trial Run_____

The first question is about the chains of attachments linking residents [10, 18–19, cf. 514], "Do you want the community to have an open social network, or should it be composed of closed social cliques?" Press "1" to select "Open social network."

The second question concerns, "How completely should people be tied together by close friendships?" You are asked to press a single number key to answer the question on a scale of 0 to 9. Zero means there will be no friendships. Nine means there will be the maximum number of friendships. This time, press "4" to get a medium number of friendships.

Now you are asked whether you want to experiment with the degree of social influence that exists between friends and acquaintances. For this part of the trial run, select "No" by pressing the "2" key.

Instantly, 112 boxes appear on the screen, representing the 112 residents of a block in Boston's Northwest End. Lines appear linking individuals who are friends. (Some lines might look dashed or dotted on your particular computer, but all lines mean a good friendship.) Neighboring boxes that are not connected by a line represent two people who are mere acquaintances. This diagram is what is called a sociogram [12] of Boston's Northwest End. One of the boxes contains a bright rectangle, indicating that this person has joined a social movement to block the destruction of the neighborhood by urban renewal.

I cannot tell you which of the 112 boxes has a bright rectangle in it. The computer has selected one at random. Also, you cannot guess ahead of time which boxes will be connected by friendship ties and which will not. The program produces about the right number implied by your command (when you typed in 4, a moment ago), but distributes them at random. Therefore, almost every run of this simulation will produce somewhat different results. Even if several students do the same laboratory assignment with this simulation, they will get a range of results, rather than all exactly the same outcome. This realistically simulates the sociology of social movements; we can state some very powerful general laws of human behavior, but the exact outcome in particular cases is determined by so many essentially random factors that prediction is difficult.

The instructions at the bottom of the screen suggest pressing RETURN/ENTER. Do so, watching what happens around the bright rectangle. Maybe nothing happens. If you look at the messages on the screen, you will see that "Week 1" of the simulation is over. Has the one member of the social movement been able to recruit somebody else? Keep pressing return until this happens.

When a member recruits a newcomer, the member's box blinks (to show you who did the recruiting), and a bright rectangle appears in the newcomer's box. A member has a much higher chance of recruiting a friend, linked by a line representing their social bond, than an acquaintance. It is possible to recruit acquaintances; it just happens much more rarely. There may be a couple of "social isolates" among the 112, people without any friendships, represented by boxes unconnected to any other. These people tend to be holdouts, reluctant to join the movement because there is nobody they trust and through whose bond they can be drawn into the growing movement. If bad luck has made the first member a social isolate, then the movement may take a long time in getting started in the community.

Press RETURN/ENTER several times more, watching as more and more people join the movement. Each week, each member is given a chance to recruit each of his or her neighbors. If you want to know which column is taking its turns at the moment, look just below the bottom boxes. You will see a line that runs under the columns of boxes, moving from left to right, pausing under each column as its members get their turns.

Announcements on the screen will keep track for you of which week it is and how many members the movement has. Continue pressing RETURN/ENTER until there are about 70 members, and the movement has recruited a majority of the community. Then Press "S" to stop the simulation.

Now you will get a self-explanatory graph of the results, showing what percent of the community were members of the movement on each week.

Press RETURN/ENTER for a table of results. This shows the membership of the movement in each week, up to a limit of 50. When you do research projects with this simulation it will give you the main results to write down for your report. Now Press RETURN/ENTER again. The computer will count how many friendships there were and what percentage this was of the total possible. This percent is the "network density."

Press RETURN/ENTER, and the run concludes with an opportunity to do it again. Press "1" so we can complete this trial run by checking out options we avoided the first time. When the program starts, select "Closed social cliques," then decide "Yes" you will experiment with the degree of social influence that exists between friends and acquaintances.

A new question appears, asking, "On a scale of 0 to 9, how much social influence should a person have over a very close friend?" Press "9" to select the highest possible influence. Had you selected "0," a member of the movement would have zero chance of recruiting his or her best friends, and the movement would fail disastrously. But we selected "9," so things look good for the movement.

Now you are given a series of options to decide how much influence a person should have over a mere acquaintance. To produce an instructive if frustrating result, select choice 6, "None at all." This means that while a member will easily recruit friends, he or she will have no luck at all recruiting people who aren't tied by a social bond.

The sociogram of the community will now appear on the screen. Notice that the boxes are connected tightly in groups of four persons. Each group member has a friendship bond with each of the other three, but no bonds with outsiders. Each group is a closed social clique.

One person in one of the cliques has joined the movement. Can you predict what will happen as you run the simulation this time? Press RETURN/ENTER several times to move forward a few weeks. Very quickly, the three other members of the clique join the movement, under the powerful influence of their friend. And that's it! Nobody else ever joins.

Projects_____

1. Study the importance of friendship bonds by comparing how fast the movement grows when there are different numbers of bonds in an open social network. Use Report Form 5 to record the number of members each week in three different experiments. The conditions for each experiment should be written in the appropriate places in the lower right corner of the form. For each of three runs, select "open social network" and choose NOT to experiment with the influence of friend versus acquaintance. Each time, use a

different number (0 through 9) to tell the computer how completely people should be tied together by close friendships.

2. In three other experiments, compare how the movement spreads through "closed social cliques" and "open social networks." Do not experiment with influence of friend versus acquaintance. On the first run, select "closed social cliques." On the second and third runs, select "open social network" and press "4" on the friendship scale of 0 to 9. This gives about the same network density you get when you choose "closed social cliques." By using the same numbers for the second and third experiments, you get the see the impact of chance in the spread of a social movement, because the results will not come out the same.

3. Experiment with different degrees of social influence between friends versus acquaintances. The three experiments could be: (1) closed social cliques, influence of friend = 5 (on the 0 to 9 scale), influence of acquaintance = 5 ("A twentieth as much"); (2) open social network, friendships = 4, influence of friend = 4; influence of acquaintance = 5; (3) open social network, friendships = 4, influence of friend = 5; influence of acquaintance = 5.

Report Form 1:
Juvenile Delinquency

☐Virginia ☐Washington

Random number: _____

NAME _____

DATE _____

Theory: _____

X: _____

	NO		YES	
	Number	Percent	Number	Percent
NO		%		%
YES		%		%

Y: _____
_____
_____

r=_____ significance=_____ gamma=_____ signif=_____

What is the relationship between the variables?

X: _____

	NO		YES	
	Number	Percent	Number	Percent
NO		%		%
YES		%		%

Y: _____
_____
_____

r=_____ significance=_____ gamma=_____ signif=_____

What is the relationship between the variables?

Report Form 2:
Births, Deaths, and Cohorts

NAME _____

DATE _____

| | YEAR | MALES | FEMALES | PERCENT OF POPULATION AGED: | | | NEW COMMAND FOR: | |
				0-4	0-19	65-99	FER-TILITY	MOR-TALITY
E X P E R I M E N T 1	0							
	20							
	40							
	60							
	80							
	100							
	120							
	140							
	160							
	180							
	200							
E X P E R I M E N T 2	0							
	20							
	40							
	60							
	80							
	100							
	120							
	140							
	160							
	180							
	200							

EXPERIMENT 1 BEGAN WITH WHICH TYPE OF SOCIETY?

EXPERIMENT 2 BEGAN WITH WHICH TYPE OF SOCIETY?

Report Form 3:
World Population Trends

NAME _____

DATE _____

NATION

YEAR	RUN STARTING FROM 1900	RUN STARTING FROM 1950	RUNS STARTING FROM 1970: CONSTANT RATE	CHANGING RATE
1950				
1960				
1970				
1980				
1990				
2000				
2010				
2020				
2030				
2040				
2050				
2060				
2070				
2080				
2090				
2100				

Report Form 4: Survey of You and Your Friends

NAME

DATE

TABLE 1:

INDEX SCORES:

A	B	C	D	E

PERCENTAGES:

A	B	C	D	E

ORTHODOXY
PARTICULARISM
RELIGIOSITY
DELINQUENCY
MALE SUBJECTS
SCIENCES
HUMANITIES
ACADEMIC

TABLE 2:

AvB	AvC	AvD	AvE	BvC

BvD	BvE	CvD	CvE	DvE

ORTHODOXY
PARTICULARISM
RELIGIOSITY
DELINQUENCY
MALE SUBJECTS
SCIENCES
HUMANITIES
ACADEMIC

TABLE 3:

AvB	AvC	AvD	AvE	BvC

COLLEGE
PREFERENCES

BvD	BvE	CvD	CvE	DvE

Report Form 5:
Boston's Northwest End

NAME

DATE

EXPERIMENT NUMBER:

WEEK	1	2	3
1			
2			
3			
4			
5			
6			
7			
8			
9			
10			
11			
12			
13			
14			
15			
16			
17			
18			
19			
20			
21			
22			
23			
24			
25			

EXPERIMENT NUMBER:

WEEK	1	2	3
26			
27			
28			
29			
30			
31			
32			
33			
34			
35			
36			
37			
38			
39			
40			
41			
42			
43			
44			
45			
46			
47			
48			
49			
50			

WRITE "C" FOR
CLOSED SOCIAL CLIQUES ➡ DENSITY OF NETWORK

NUMBER OF FRIENDSHIPS

LEAVE BLANK IF
YOU ARE NOT ➡ INFLUENCE ON FRIEND
EXPERIMENTING ➡ INFLUENCE ON ACQUAINTANCE
WITH INFLUENCE